About HP

HP is the world's largest technology company operating in more than 170 countries around the world. We explore how technology and services can help people and companies address their problems and challenges, and realise their possibilities, aspirations and dreams. We apply new thinking and ideas to create more simple, valuable and trusted experiences with technology, continuously improving the way our customers live and work. For public sector organisations that want to improve efficiency and provide greater access to information, people and processes while reducing costs, HP combines the full breadth of its portfolio and alliances, as well as extensive worldwide experience and industry-standard technologies to create and deliver cost-effective, innovative solutions.

About Demos

Who we are

Demos is the think tank for everyday democracy. We believe everyone should be able to make personal choices in their daily lives that contribute to the common good. Our aim is to put this democratic idea into practice by working with organisations in ways that make them more effective and legitimate.

What we work on

We focus on seven areas: public services; science and technology; cities and public space; people and communities; families and care; arts and culture; and global security.

Who we work with

Our partners include policy-makers, companies, public service providers and social entrepreneurs. Demos is not linked to any party but we work with politicians across political divides. Our international network – which extends across Eastern Europe, Scandinavia, Australia, Brazil, India and China – provides a global perspective and enables us to work across borders.

How we work

Demos knows the importance of learning from experience. We test and improve our ideas in practice by working with people who can make change happen. Our collaborative approach means that our partners share in the creation and ownership of new ideas.

What we offer

We analyse social and political change, which we connect to innovation and learning in organisations. We help our partners show thought leadership and respond to emerging policy challenges.

How we communicate

As an independent voice, we can create debates that lead to real change. We use the media, public events, workshops and publications to communicate our ideas. All our books can be downloaded free from the Demos website.

www.demos.co.uk

First published in 2007
© Demos
Some rights reserved – see copyright licence for details

ISBN 978 1 84180 182 7
Copy edited by Julie Pickard, London
Typeset by utimestwo, Collingtree, Northants
Printed by IPrint, Leicester

For further information and
subscription details please contact:

Demos
Magdalen House
136 Tooley Street
London SE1 2TU

telephone: 0845 458 5949
email: hello@demos.co.uk
web: www.demos.co.uk

Unlocking Innovation
Why citizens hold the key to
public service reform

Edited by
Sophia Parker
Simon Parker

DEM⊙S

DEM⊝S

Open access. Some rights reserved.

Contents

Contents

Acknowledgements

We are grateful to HP for supporting this work. In particular, we would like to thank Rob Watt, Brian Fenix and David Abrahams for their patience, support and encouragement throughout the project process. Thanks are also due to the talented and generous people who made the time to contribute essays.

Many others have helped to produce and edit this collection. Tom Bentley put the project together and has been a constant source of support and advice throughout. Faizal Farook and Niamh Gallagher provided invaluable editorial support. Peter Harrington and Julie Pickard deftly managed the production process. Charlie Edwards, Duncan O'Leary and Shelagh Wright kindly provided comments on early drafts of the essays.

Sophia Parker
Simon Parker
June 2007

Foreword

Ed Miliband

This pamphlet draws our attention to a range of important challenges, but one particularly stands out: the need to create truly collaborative public services, which allow users and communities to work with professionals and institutions to shape and contribute to them.

Why is this so important? Because so much expertise about what makes for effective public services lies with the user – whether that is a homeless teenager, a patient with diabetes or a parent-governor of a school. And so many of the challenges we face in public services – from chronic disease to success in education – cannot be properly tackled without engagement and contributions from patients, pupils and parents.

Sometimes users will do this individually, sometimes collectively. This is because public services are not like private services that just happen to be provided outside the marketplace, but are often inherently collective, from youth services to schools to the local environment. Many are about our shared experiences and our common bonds. They both require and can benefit from accountability to a community of users.

There are many examples of user and collective involvement on which we can build. Sometimes we see the idea of a rigid divide between professionals and users being broken down. The Expert Patient programme run by the Department of Health, for example, enables those suffering from chronic disease to help others to cope with their condition. In other cases, the involvement of users is about their ability to shape collectively the kind of services they want to see, as with youth capital budgets being allocated locally by young people.

This collection points the way forward to other examples of user-led innovation and to some lessons we can learn. Simon Duffy shows how recent changes in social care have empowered users to improve their quality of life. Chris Naylor highlights the potential of a user focus to drive innovation in local authorities and Sophia Parker calls for a public sector that invests more systematically in the role of users as drivers for innovative public services.

Crucially, involving users and communities must not be an excuse for the withdrawal of the state – a form of 'DIY welfare' in which patients get less support and local services get less funding. In fact, as we look around and see that our society still has injustice, inequality and unmet needs, we know that we need to mobilise users and communities in the interests of more and better services, not services on the cheap.

Genuinely supporting the involvement of users and communities is a way to bring about a higher quality of service, a stronger public realm, and the flow of innovative ideas that this pamphlet rightly identifies as necessary. It means that across public services we need to strengthen the scope for input from users, improve the opportunities for collective accountability for local services and strengthen the ability of frontline staff to be sources of innovation and collaboration.

This collection is an important contribution to this process of learning and I commend the lessons it can teach us. I hope it furthers the debate about innovation and the role of users in public services. As we look ahead, both are central to creating the kind of public services and society we want to see.

Introduction

Sophia Parker and Simon Parker

At different points in the last 200 years the UK has undergone dramatic bursts of economic and institutional innovation. From becoming the cradle of the industrial innovation, to the formation of the welfare state, to the emergence of an open, service-driven economy through Thatcherism, spurts of change have shaped much longer societal trajectories. Over the next 20 years, we need a similar reorientation of our public services. This collection is about the kinds of innovation, and the strategies for harnessing it, that are needed to achieve that shift successfully.

Together, the essays included here argue that we need to renew and refocus our understanding of innovation. Rather than simply driving change through new processes, better technology and the imposition of good practice from above, we need increasingly to look to the everyday interactions between people and public services for new ideas. Governments need to move from a model based on predicting needs and producing plans to meet them, to one based on meeting needs in real time through participation and co-production.

Change in the public sector is critical – schools, hospitals and councils already account for 20 per cent of our GDP and a range of social trends are increasing the pressure for still more spending. A population whose needs will be increasingly chronic or long term – either through illness or age – will place unprecedented demands on a welfare state designed for a previous age where the primary goal was to alleviate crises and provide treatments and cures. Even on the most optimistic projections, NHS spending will have to rise from 9.4 per cent to 10.6 per cent of GDP to keep pace in the 2020s – equivalent to £56 billion extra in 2002 prices.[1]

This kind of spending increase will be difficult at a time when the legitimacy of public services is in jeopardy. Rising demands, finite resources and some of the lowest levels of trust in government in Europe[2] have combined to create a gap between what the public expects and what institutions can deliver. New approaches to politics and service delivery are the only credible way to close this gap.

This problem of legitimacy is compounded by the complexity of some of the social challenges facing the UK, and a growing sense that quality of life is not improving along with incomes and public spending. This sense was symbolised by a recent Unicef report that named Britain as having the worst levels of childhood wellbeing in the developed world.[3] As things get better overall, the most complex problems remain and therefore stand out even more starkly than before.

The challenges facing our current models of public service provision are significant, but they are not insoluble. Much is improving, and there are many more tools and methods available to tackle what feel like intractable problems. A major driver, still under-exploited in public services, is the impact of information technology. The combination of a more educated and empowered populace and the explosion of new ways of sharing information and working collaboratively has the potential to transform the nature and boundaries of the public sector.

As Rob Watt and David Varney argue in their essays, the new models for citizen collaboration offered by technology mean that ideas that seemed unlikely only a generation ago are suddenly becoming real possibilities. When Ivan Illich made the case for 'de-schooling' society in the 1970s it was a radical idea and there were few tools to make it happen.[4] Today, technology is enabling us to learn almost anywhere – for example through online learning and reciprocal exchange of skills and knowledge – in ways that Illich could barely have imagined.

From delivery chains to co-production

Government seemed so much simpler in 1997. Public services had suffered from over a decade of low investment, the people who worked in them were demoralised and startling gaps in equality of opportunity and outcome could no longer be ignored. New Labour was elected on a ticket of 'renewal', which was to be delivered through a package of discrete, measurable interventions such as reducing class sizes and waiting lists.

A new generation of Labour ministers adopted the language of management consultancy and pursued a particular organisational metaphor: that of the machine. They sought to make the task of public service reform one of rational, scientific analysis, arguing that improvement could be wrought through better use of Whitehall's key 'levers of change' – essentially legislation and performance management – and a stronger evidence base for 'what works', regardless of ideology.

In 2007 the picture is rather different. The metaphor of the machine – the idea of predictable, rational, cause and effect analysis, may have brought about some significant improvements, but it has also failed to tackle deeper questions of motivation and legitimacy. Public sector staff are disengaged and frustrated. Citizens, while positive about their personal experiences of services, remain stubbornly disillusioned with standards overall.

The government's performance indicators and inspection scores often bear little relation to the way people experience and perceive the services they receive. So ministers end up seeing the world differently from citizens, and the gulf between the two views seems to be filling with cynicism about the capacity of the state to improve people's lives.

In this environment, policy-makers are increasingly recognising that they need a new range of approaches to create change. 'Co-production', 'personalisation', 'empowerment' and 'engagement' are concepts that have flown the seminar room and are now discussed openly in Whitehall, even if few people really know how to put them into practice. There is a level of interest in frontline innovation that has not been seen since the late 1990s.

The search for a new narrative of public service reform has already begun. Politicians and their advisers are seeking a new approach to improvement that moves beyond the prescriptive systems of targets, inspections and markets, and reconnects to people – who they are, what motivates them and how they really tend to behave. Successful public service reform needs to invest more in people's own capabilities, and share responsibility with them for producing better outcomes, without simply dumping risk onto individuals.

Yet the alliance for change remains fragile. The operating system of government is still dominated by the new public management, expensive consultants and notions of delivery chains that start with policy and end with a one-dimensional 'customer'. A shift of language and aspiration is not enough to reorient the substance of how government works. New tools, practices, organising frameworks and sources of disruption are needed.

Making that reorientation happen in practice is a political as well as managerial imperative. The main parties cannot sustain themselves for the next decade with more promises of technical improvements to public institutions. The agenda is shifting under their feet, as opinion polls show the public increasingly worried about broad social issues such as crime, immigration and security.[5] The political response should be a new discourse about the role of government in helping society to address those problems. Rather than claiming to have the answers, politicians will need to encourage a more investigative, innovative attitude – working with citizens to try new things and find out what works.

That approach will require policy-makers to take a very different view of the way that innovation happens, engaging with new challenges and opportunities and using them as a spur to fundamentally redesign our public services. Ultimately, this means moving beyond process innovation – delivering the same thing better

– to outcome-based innovation, which might mean delivering something entirely different to better meet social needs.

The locus of innovation

Innovation is a word so overused that it is in danger of losing any conceptual clarity. We see it here as a simple concept: 'learning to do things differently, to do them better'. But while the concept is simple, the way we try to support and develop innovation is not. As Jonathan Kestenbaum, chief executive of NESTA, recently argued:

> *Innovation is frequently found in unlikely places. It is rarely based on traditional understandings of linear, 'pipeline' research and development that lead only to new products, drugs or technology.*[6]

And yet the idea of public sector innovation emerging from a well-structured 'pipeline' of research and development still has a strong hold on the collective imagination of government. Surveying the landscape of innovation policy it becomes clear that government's efforts to discover and promote better outcomes rest on a series of limited and increasingly outdated assumptions about how innovation really occurs – for instance that:

○　new solutions are mostly developed in the offices of Whitehall, the departments of universities, and the R&D functions of large technology firms – where the role of public servants on the ground is simply to find the best approach to implementation
○　innovation grows out of major hardware solutions implemented at scale, and business process re-engineering
○　process innovation (or 'lean systems') is the most effective way of improving efficiency, particularly when it reduces the amount of money lost in the delivery chain between Whitehall and the frontline and cuts back-office costs

O   government fully understands the nature of our
     problems, so just needs innovation in the development
     of solutions
O   evels of innovative activity can be measured by
     investment in scientific and technical invention alone
O   innovation is driven only by market or quasi-market
     competition.

It is true that operational innovations – innovations that take place
within the defined parameters of current systems of service – can
make a real difference. But really transformative changes are far more
likely to emerge from changing the interactions between services and
people. So innovation needs to become far more than a way to meet a
target or design the cost out of a process. Truly effective innovations
will be those that find new ways of meeting existing needs and
responding to those that are currently unmet. They will also be those
that harness the energies and motivations of the public themselves in
helping to define and solve their own problems.

Achieving and sustaining these effects across large, complex sectors
and among millions of people requires a more ambitious and
rigorous understanding of how innovative activities can be connected
and spread through whole systems of organisations.

Successful innovation systems vary widely across different
countries. But they tend to share two distinguishing characteristics.
First, the recognition that consistent production of new knowledge
requires sustained public investment in innovation. Second, an
understanding that the systems which enable successful application of
knowledge cut across traditional organisational and sectoral
boundaries, both within government and between the public sector
and the wider economy.

As Tom Bentley argues in this collection, there are five key
functions that underpin effective innovation systems:

O   identifying opportunities
O   creating and distributing knowledge and capabilities

○ supporting and financing new organisations and
production capacities
○ managing risk and uncertainty
○ creating and managing infrastructures.

Championing innovation in the future will mean developing these
capabilities within whole sectors of service provision – helping the
health or education systems, for instance, to successfully generate and
disseminate their own innovation, rather than relying on
conventional models of central government transferring best practice.

Recognising the hidden innovators

In Whitehall, at least, innovation is still largely driven by top-down
approaches, where the focus is often on senior civil servants
implementing new systems or ways of measuring performance.[7] And
yet research repeatedly underlines the fact that new ideas are more
likely to emerge at the interface between public servants and the
people they serve. One major review demonstrated that 85 per cent of
public service innovations were developed by frontline staff or their
managers.[8] But because these innovations often happen in isolated
pockets a long way from the centre of government, they tend to go
unrecognised. While they remain invisible, isolated and unquantified,
it will be impossible to construct a coherent policy agenda for
supporting, sustaining and investing in such hidden innovations.

If they are serious about a reform agenda that is both effective and
legitimate, then governments need to invest more time and money in
this kind of frontline, people-centred innovation. If deployed as a
coherent strategy, this investment should generate a multiplier effect
– once the conditions for user-driven innovation are established, they
should yield a stream of new ideas based on better and deeper
insights into people's needs.

The essays collected here offer some basic design principles for a
strategy that could support a system-wide shift to people-centred
innovation. Taken together, they point towards five key transforma-
tions.

1. From process-led to demand-led innovation

Innovation needs to start with people's needs, rather than limiting itself to the fixed parameters of existing service provision. Simon Duffy's essay explores the impact of a 'person-centred support' model of social care. One participant in the early pilot of this model described her experience: 'It's not a service I want, it is a lifestyle.' At the local authority level, Chris Naylor's essay outlines the importance of designing services around the needs of users, and the potential implications for councils. Allowing users to articulate their own needs and aspirations, and creating incentives for service providers to respond, is a potent source both of specific innovations and of pressure to learn and adapt faster.

2. From solution-centred to problem-centred innovation

The culture of government is often to spend something like 20 per cent of its time defining the problem, and 80 per cent of its time implementing the solution. We need a better balance. Harnessing the perspective of users implies a more careful approach to problem definition, and the ability to reconfigure the organisational frame-work through which government tries to deliver solutions. Mapping, diagnosing and modelling the interrelated elements of problems to be solved is essential for tackling complex challenges, not least because it enables service users and professionals to agree on what the problem is in the first place. Ian Keys and Roger O'Sullivan argue that public–private partnerships increasingly need to be based on precisely this process of defining and redefining the problem, rather than contracting for predefined solutions. Jack Stilgoe and Faizal Farook show in their essay how better conversations between health professionals and patients can help to assess needs better and create better solutions. Melissa Mean shows how this approach can be taken forward at the scale of a whole city.

3. From best practice to next practices

Many of the government's highest-profile policies have taken an approach to innovation based on seeking out and endorsing good practices before trying to spread them uniformly across hundreds of organisations. Rather than simply spreading existing practice, we need to encourage and prototype new approaches that challenge existing paradigms. Sophia Parker examines how user-led approaches to change can generate radical innovations across whole sectors, as well as incremental improvements in individual organisations. Similarly, Geoff Mulgan and Simon Tucker outline an approach to taking local innovations to scale based on identifying promising practices, developing and scaling them up through repeated iterations of design, delivery and feedback. And Tom Bentley reflects on what such models could mean at the level of the whole government system. His essay illustrates the contours of a system that can learn from itself, continuously and sustainably.

4. From managerial to relational models

'What matters is what works' is one of the defining phrases of Blair's premiership. But who decides what works? Heavily managerial approaches have privileged scientific, quantifiable evidence over the public's everyday experiences. Mette Abrahamsen's essay explains how Denmark has attempted to introduce a more creative approach into its government ministries – bringing new skills and approaches to deciding 'what works' into the heart of the central bureaucracy. David Varney's essay makes the case for an approach to efficiency that starts with the interaction between people and services, rather than the internal workings of that service alone.

5. From information to interaction

The spread of web 2.0 technologies based on social networking allows us to create genuinely new kinds of connection between people and public services. Often it is our children, not the senior policy-makers, who know most about this potential. Keri Facer and Hannah Green's essay explores how children are demonstrating a massive untapped potential as contributors to service design – they show us how much the education system could learn from its own pupils. Rob Watt's essay outlines what such insights might mean at the level of national government in terms of commissioning, procuring and implementing new technology to engage people in the common goal of improving outcomes.

Innovative ecosystems

Within the public sector, there are already pockets of activity that reflect this emerging understanding of innovation. One legacy of New Labour is a wider range of providers involved in service delivery and support, creating a potential for far more productive diversity. The question is whether all this energy can be harnessed with enough policy and regulation to discipline its direction, but not so much that it is strangled. Government needs to find ways to convert innovation systematically into better outcomes and greater capacity to learn and adapt to change.

This means policy-makers shifting further from an approach to governing that often seems like driving a car or flying a plane with a cockpit full of instruments to tending a more complex but partially self-organising ecosystem. In an interdependent world, innovation won't happen simply because we demand or incentivise it. Instead, it will emerge when different tiers of government align their motivations, values and activities in a search for solutions.

Developing more people-focused kinds of innovation will also require policy-makers to take into account a wider range of information and evidence. Economic and performance data tells us only part of the story when it comes to public services – if we want to redesign them around people's needs, we have to understand more about the way people themselves see and experience those needs. Social science and systems analysis need to become a much greater part of the evidence base at all levels of government.

We have argued in this introduction that human-centred innovation – innovation at the 'interface' – is the form of activity most likely to yield better outcomes. The first section of this pamphlet therefore explores what innovation at the interface looks like in practice. However, innovations at the interface will remain there unless more work is done to create a better alignment between the other equally important elements of the system. The remaining three sections of the collection examine innovation at other levels: the local, the strategic centre, and the systems and infrastructure of government.

At the heart of this pamphlet is the argument that we need a richer view of innovation and a public policy environment that does not treat it as something that happens in a discrete unit or through one-off projects, but rather as something that needs to be nurtured as part of the agenda to create public services that are able to learn and adapt as the world around them changes. As with government, innovation is an art rather than a science.

Notes

1   D Wanless, *Securing our Future Health: Taking a long-term view* (London: HM Treasury, 2002), available at www.hm-treasury.gov.uk/consultations_and_legislation/wanless/consult_wanless_final.cfm (accessed 11 Apr 2007).
2   Only 24% of people in the UK trust the government, making the country joint 23rd lowest out of the EU25. This position is held jointly with France. Eurobarometer 66. National Report: United Kingdom, available at: http://ec.europa.eu/public_opinion/archives/eb/eb66/eb66_uk_nat.pdf (accessed 11 Apr 2007).
3   Unicef, *Child Poverty in Perspective: An overview of child wellbeing in rich countries* (Florence: Unicef, 2007), available at http://news.bbc.co.uk/nol/shared/bsp/hi/pdfs/13_02_07_nn_unicef.pdf (accessed 18 Jun 2007).
4   I Illich, *De-schooling Society* (Suffolk: Marion Boyars, 2000).
5   Ipsos Mori political monitor, July 2006, available at www.ipsos-mori.com/polls/2006/mpm060724.shtml (accessed 12 Jun 2007).
6   Foreword to NESTA, *The Innovation Gap: Why policy needs to reflect the reality of innovation in the UK* (London: National Endowment for Science, Technology and the Arts, 2006), available at www.nesta.org.uk/assets/pdf/innovation_gap_report_NESTA.pdf (accessed 11 Apr 2007).
7   National Audit Office, *Achieving Innovation in Central Government Organisations* (London: TSO, Jul 2006), available at www.nao.org.uk/publications/nao_reports/05-06/05061447i.pdf (accessed 12 Jun 2007).
8   S Borins, *The Challenge of Innovating in Government*, 2nd edn (Toronto: IBM Centre for the Business of Government, University of Toronto, 2006).

Essay summaries

Interfaces
Participative public services
Simon Duffy

However hard current models of social care are worked, they will never be able to cope with the nature and scale of demand emerging in the early years of the twenty-first century. A new model should begin by telling people exactly what their care budget is. This apparently small shift has seismic implications. People who know their own budget are able not only to consider existing services, but also alternatives that they may find preferable.

Curriculum 2.0
Keri Facer and Hannah Green

As children become more technologically literate, gaining access to more sources of learning and information, we need to create bridges between what they are learning in school and what they are learning out of school, and between the skills they are acquiring in the classroom and those they will need to thrive throughout their lives. Rather than rejecting the possibilities offered by the internet, we need to isolate and build on the positive aspects of young people's experiences in a formal setting.

Doctor, the patient will see you now

Jack Stilgoe and Faizal Farook

For all the effort expended on a particular kind of 'modernisation' of the health service over the past decade, it is notable that most of the innovation has focused on new technology and management systems. The everyday conversations between healthcare professionals and the people they serve have been relatively neglected, despite the fact that these conversations are where government policy, new technology and patient needs meet. An innovative health service needs to have better conversations that allow its users to define the terms of participation.

Localities

Localism and innovation

Paul Coen and Matthew Warburton

Local government needs to learn how to spread innovation across the sector faster and better without relying on Whitehall. For many years, councils have complained about the 'tyranny of best practice' – the predilection of government to alight on innovative practice, anoint it with official support and insist it is applied everywhere without regard to variation in local needs or circumstances. Now we have to show we can do better.

Customer-driven service design

Chris Naylor

We needed to improve customer satisfaction with our services, but we quickly recognised that this would depend on a better understanding of who our customers were and how they wanted to interact with us. Our new approach has not come solely from within the council, but from a deeper engagement with the people we serve – the explicit aim of our new improvement strategy is to become 'customer-led'.

Urban innovation and the power of mass imagination

Melissa Mean

Our faith in cities has been restored over the past decade, but the existing formula for urban innovation is starting to look stale. A new pattern of innovation is emerging that is open and distributed – an ecology rather than a pipeline. Instead of an elite activity occurring only in special places, it needs to involve many players and needs to take root in diverse clusters of places and spaces, drawing on both location and imagination. This is potentially an incredibly democratic and empowering story.

Innovation in public–private partnerships

Ian Keys and Roger O'Sullivan

Despite the rhetoric, innovation in public–private partnerships is actually quite rare. Enabling it requires a new approach that involves early dialogue between potential partners and more flexible relationships between the public and private sectors that allow the service to be developed dynamically. Such an approach involves risks for all players, but the rewards are worthwhile. Tight contracts behind which both sides hide when the going gets tough will become a thing of the past and a more flexible, responsive and public-value-based model will emerge.

The strategic centre

Twenty-first-century civil servants

Mette Abrahamsen

In the Danish Ministry of Economic and Business Affairs, we constantly try to encourage innovation across the economy, but we also wanted to encourage new practices and ideas within our own institution. So we created MindLab, a space in the ministry which could not only symbolise innovation in itself, but actually foster real, practical innovation among civil servants. More specifically, we wanted to support innovation throughout the ministry by facilitating the early and most vulnerable phases of projects.

Reforming through technology

Rob Watt

There are two well-established approaches to innovation in

government – some policy changes try to improve the effectiveness of service outcomes, others are aimed primarily at improving productivity and efficiency. But there is a third and under-exploited form of innovation: the public sector should also be involved in developing its own disruptive new technological innovations, changing the rules of public service reform rather than just playing the game more effectively.

Transforming government
David Varney

In recent years we have seen a number of initiatives focused on increasing efficiency and productivity in our public services. Most of these have concentrated on 'back office', business process redesign and shared services agendas rather than the 'front end' of services – the contact and interactions between services and people's lives. My argument is that, through the innovative use of technology, we can drive further efficiencies *and* improved service experiences by transforming the 'front end' of services, as well as the back office.

Systems of governing
Porous government
Sophia Parker

Investing systematically in user-driven innovation in the public sector has huge implications for models of management and for the processes by which policy is developed and implemented. Government will need to become more porous, letting people into previously closed systems of policy-making. It may feel counterintuitive to those sitting in Whitehall offices, but in order to gain legitimacy they will need to be willing to give up more power to the public and to let service users into policy development cycles at much earlier stages.

Scaling up innovation
Geoff Mulgan and Simon Tucker

Scaling up local inventions should not be an inherent problem for governments that have the power, money and ability to enact legislation that can make things happen on a large scale relatively easily. Yet time and again successful small, local initiatives fail to break into the mainstream. This seems to be a perennial issue, for, without the ability to bring innovations to scale, governments cannot take advantage of innovation as the most important driver of quality and relevance in public services.

Seven kinds of learning
Tom Bentley

To succeed in the twenty-first century, governments will need to learn faster and more deeply from innovation. They can do this without changing their core identities, by working out how to learn continuously through the iterative cycles of their ongoing routines, rather than simply making incremental steps forward. Judging what to do on the basis of imperfect information is the essence of both political and organisational leadership. Those leaders who build learning systems around their routines will be the ones who do most to help reinvent government for the twenty-first century.

Interfaces

1. Participative public services

Innovation through redistributing power
Simon Duffy

Historically, 'social care' is a term that has been used to cover a wide range of public service support – the 'caring services' offered to disabled people, older people and people with mental health problems. The services on offer to these groups are defined primarily by a history of institutional oppression and, in some cases, the self-serving interests of professional groups, rather than by the aspirations and lifestyles of the groups being served. In this sense, social care is the starkest example of a wider truth about public services: its users are defined as passive recipients. They get what the service decides is right for them, and there are few or no opportunities to shape that service.

Social care also exemplifies another classic problem that limits the ability of public services to meet our needs as 'whole' people. Budgets to support chronic conditions are utterly fragmented. In the UK, £22 billion is spent through disability benefits; £19 billion is spent through budgets for adult and children's social care; £1.5 billion is channelled through the Supporting People programme; approximately £20 billion of NHS money will be spent on supporting people with long-term conditions. In addition to this there are numerous other pots of money such as the Independent Living Fund. Such fragmentation, with its accompanying rules, ring fences, accountability chains and timescales, make the goal of person-centred support almost unachievable.

While this position may be sustainable for now, projections about the population's health and demand for social care suggest it cannot be long before the care sector becomes a major political headache. We know that already the NHS spends around 80 per cent of its total budget on chronic disease, which also accounts for roughly 60 per cent of hospital bed days. Some 80 per cent of GP consultations are about chronic disease.[1]

From diabetes to depression, from chronic heart conditions to longer life expectancy, we are on the cusp of an epidemic in chronic conditions that will force the question: how can such exponential rises in demand be met by a system designed to deal with acute health issues and not much more?

The only innovations that will work in this context will need to focus on how to bring more resources (time and energy, as well as cold cash) into the system. However hard current models are worked, they will never be able to cope with the nature and scale of demand emerging in the early years of the twenty-first century.

The moral case for more participation

Think back to the last time you had to stay in a hospital for a few days. Remember how institutionalised and weakened you can become in an environment where others are clearly in control. For some people, this subjection to the power and control of others is a 24 hours a day, 7 days a week experience. The emphasis on passive recipients that is 'hardwired' into our systems of public service reaches its worst extreme when services are offered to groups who are already marginalised, poor or subject to prejudice. Even though many of the old models of long-stay institutions have disappeared, the services that have replaced them have stayed firmly within the same historical pattern:

- O   day centres, where people spend their day removed from both their home and the full range of possible community resources
- O   special transport, which moves people between day

    centres and their homes, minimising contact with other
    citizens
- group homes, care homes or nursing homes, where people
  live with other people they have not chosen to live with,
  supported by staff they do not control
- even the domicillary services that have been developed to
  offer people support at home are largely controlled by
  contractual arrangements that leave the person with no
  discretion over how and when they are supported.

For many years now, the disability movement has campaigned hard
for a 'citizenship model' for public services – in other words a model
that recognises the right to independence, dignity and respect that is a
basic part of everyone's human rights. The citizenship model offers a
vastly different vision of social care from our current picture: a vision
which refocuses power and responsibility with the disabled person at
the centre of their own network of family and friends. It promises a
system in which people are treated as active citizens, not passive
recipients.

The rhetoric of participation, consultation and involvement has
been with us a long while, and it has intensified in recent years under
a government that has advocated ever-greater 'choice and voice' as a
key driver for more innovation and better services.

However, there is a gap between rhetoric and reality, and nowhere
is this gap more pronounced than in social care services. Meaningful
participation is simply not possible while there is no political will to
alter current systems of power, responsibility and money. Figure 1
describes how power would need to shift to enable genuine power to
rest with the individual rather than the service.

The emergence of in Control

In 2003, a small group of people came together to form a programme
called in Control, with the specific aim of developing and testing a
profoundly new way of working, which we call 'Self-Directed
Support'.[2]

Figure 1 Shifting power to the individual

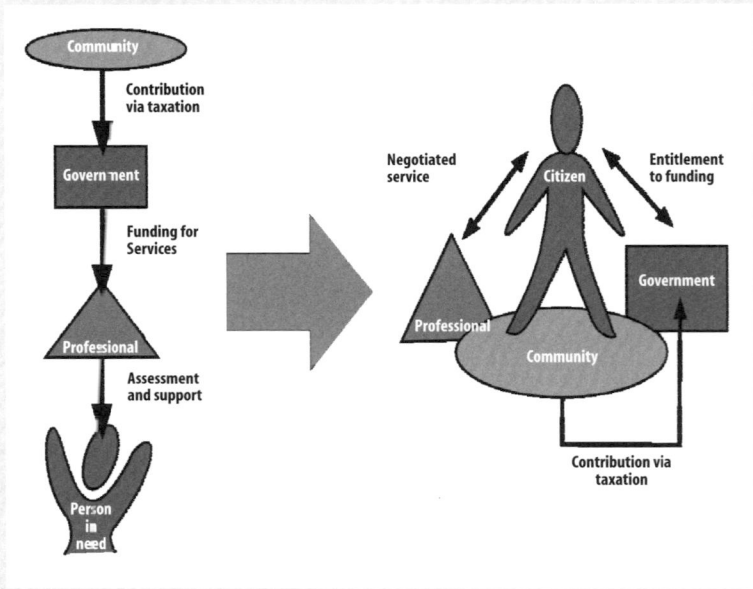

Source: in Control

Our belief was that more person-centred approaches to social care were morally right. We also believed that such a model of social care might be the only hope of creating forms of support able to meet the demands likely to be placed on the future system. Our hunch – informed by early, very local prototypes of our model – was that person-centred approaches might not only improve people's lives, and their sense of autonomy, but that they would also prove to be more sustainable in the long run, and represent a better means of allocating resources that will inevitably be limited.

The remainder of this essay tells the story of in Control, our work since 2003 to develop and refine our model, and our efforts to spread a new 'operating system' for social care. In our system, people become participants in shaping, commissioning and delivering their care rather than passive, dependent and sometimes vulnerable and confused recipients of what the existing model deems them to be eligible for.

We are under no illusions: the scale of change implied by our person-centred support model is enormous. But our vision is to understand how to use our innovative model of person-centred support to drive change, so that participative approaches to social care become the norm over the next three to five years.

Turning assessment on its head

There are already some models for personalising support in social care in the UK through putting people in control of their budgets – for example the Independent Living Fund and Direct Payments. However, these models cover only a tiny proportion of overall care budgets, and exclude those people with more complex needs. In Control's aim is to build a universal system – Self-Directed Support – that could work for everyone.

The limits of the current system and its inability to build supple, flexible, person-centred services is exemplified by the assessment process:

○ A care manager will assess each person on the basis of a means test where your chances of receiving support are significantly increased if you are poor, if you have few social assets, and if your life is in crisis. For a growing number of councils, it is only if you fit these criteria that you can access any services at all – creating an incentive to escalate needs.
○ The individual has no independent sense of what they are entitled to, other than via this professionally led process – creating a positive incentive for that individual to present their needs in terms of the services that they are aware of.

Figure 2 The current assessment process

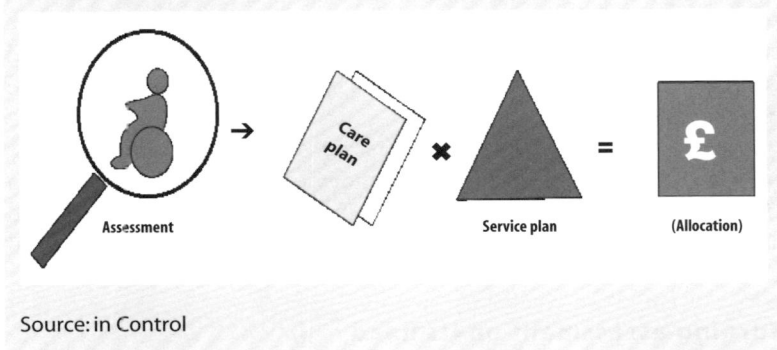

Source: in Control

O   The care manager will work with the individual to
    develop a care plan, but the amount of funding available
    is not clear at this stage. The care manager then has to
    negotiate with a panel which is charged with making
    rationing decisions. The care manager may have to make
    several attempts to get the plan 'through' the panel. At no
    point is there real clarity about the amount of money
    actually available to the client.

O   Finally, most social care spending is pre-committed to
    blocks of services that are commissioned with little or no
    reference to individual needs, meaning that even if a
    person qualifies for support, what the care manager can
    offer is seriously constrained by a set of decisions that
    have often been made on the basis of an institutional
    history of welfare.

The failure of the current system to involve or empower people is
inevitable while such an assessment process is in place – this process
is set out in figure 2.

   It was therefore at the assessment stage that the in Control model
began to imagine an alternative vision of social care, defined by

Figure 3 The in Control assessment process

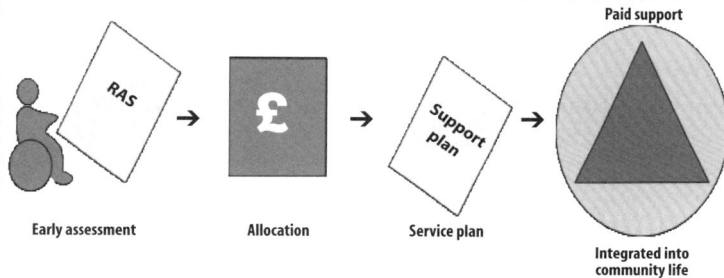

Source: in Control

reconfigured power relationships that we 'designed in' to our own assessment approach. We turned this entire process on its head, aiming for a better connection of the rules that match funding with needs. We call this our 'Resource Allocation System'. It is not only more efficient in itself, but it also begins to radically empower the disabled person and those around them.

It is a simple idea. The in Control model begins by telling people exactly what their budget is, regardless of any other factors such as access to support from friends and family and so on – it is set out in figure 3.

This apparently small shift has seismic implications. People who know their own budget are able not only to consider existing services, but also alternatives that they may find preferable. Friends and families can negotiate their own contribution to social care support without fear that these decisions will alter the amount of state support an individual can access. The relationship between the care manager, the individual and their family can rest on honesty, on a shared goal of finding the best way of spending that budget, rather than on a power relationship where the care manager has more weight than the individual in determining service and resource allocation. Finally, as people are working out how to spend their budget, they can get help in making decisions from people other than the care manager.

A new idea . . . that works

The impact of this new approach in practice has been very positive. The early evaluations[3] suggest that:

○ people are more satisfied with their lives and with the services they receive (eg satisfaction with support went from 48 per cent to 100 per cent)
○ people feel more in control of their life and achieve more of their own goals (eg people achieved 79 per cent of their specific goals in less than one year)
○ people tend to choose less institutional forms of services, although not every change is made at once and some people continue to use more traditional services (eg everyone left residential care, but day service usage dropped by only 22 per cent)
○ it is less wasteful, with early aggregate efficiencies of the order of 20 per cent.

The government is now showing increasing interest in these ideas and has developed the Individual Budget Pilot Programme in order to test them further.[4] Local authorities have also become more interested and 85 local authorities have now joined in Control in order to implement its Self-Directed Support model.

A new operating system: scaling up our innovation

Of course the real challenge for in Control is not to develop a better way of organising social care, but to find ways of encouraging the existing system and the individuals who operate within it or depend on it to shift their behaviour. In Control has had little access to central authority, nor does it have significant resources. It has had to rely on the innate attractiveness and coherence of the concept of Self-

Directed Support. In order to find a way of communicating these ideas as powerfully as possible in Control borrowed a number of key concepts from the world of computers and the internet:

1   Self-Directed Support has been developed as a new operating system for social care, a system that can be integrated into local communities and local systems in order to better achieve citizenship for disabled people.

2   In Control's materials are published on the internet as Open Source freeware, available for adaptation and further development by local leaders.

3   In Control focuses on making its materials accessible and easy to use in order to make implementation as simple as possible.

4   In Control uses an editorial process to make iterative improvements to the model and publish new versions of the model regularly.[5]

5   The operating system has been designed to be backward compatible, which means that instead of competing with the older system the model can be implemented in a way that integrates with the more conservative practices that some may still want or need.[6]

6   The system is universal – it can be applied to everyone who uses social care. This encourages serious and significant implementation and helps to stop innovations being treated as marginal and just for a 'chosen few'.

7   The system may also be extendable, for one of the exciting possibilities of this approach is that it offers a way of capturing some of the diverse funding streams that have been developed for disabled people but which are often lost within complex bureaucratic systems, with additional administrative costs and subject to overlapping or contradictory sets of rules.[7]

8   It also seems sustainable, although the economics of Self-Directed Support are complex.[8] The greater efficiency of

this approach is no guarantee of success when there are
significant vested interests at stake and where a new
system can be overtaken by previously unmet needs when
resources locked into older forms of provision have not
been released. However, in Control has continued to
invest energy in ensuring that local authorities develop
resource allocation systems that can allow them to
manage the process of change while ensuring the benefits
of this approach are rolled out to greater numbers.

So, to begin with, in Control defined and published its model of Self-
Directed Support based on the available national and international
evidence of what was working and on its own analysis of why the
current system and previous innovations had not worked. In
addition, the operating system was made sensitive to the challenges of
implementation at the local level. In particular, it was important to
ensure that people implementing the system knew that:

○   they were working within existing laws and policies
○   they were able to manage within existing resources
○   they could interpret the operating system locally and
    make their own innovations
○   the proposed system was an internally coherent and
    attractive alternative approach.

While these may seem modest constraints it is not uncommon for
policy-makers and innovators to pay too little attention to these kinds
of issues. Local authorities and service providers have often found, for
example, that the financial impact of new systems has not been
considered or that there is a significant tension between a new system
and other rules that operate within the system. So, working in this
way, sensitive to these constraints, builds support and legitimacy at
the local level.

A further benefit of this approach is its permissiveness, the fact
that it is left open to local interpretation and encourages coherent

innovations which can then be built into the model or enable radical revisions to the model. Many of the innovations that have been developed have arisen by local people applying the model, finding problems and developing better solutions.

The role of the centre in distributed innovation

It also turns out, although this was perhaps a more unexpected benefit of this approach, that developing a coherent alternative narrative for social care has enabled a greater willingness at the level of central government to consider radical change.[9] The relationship between central government and local innovators is typically hampered by a number of key factors:

○ Central government has a low understanding of how local communities work and how central policies are actually implemented, and there is a significant lag time before policy-makers understand how their policies are being implemented.
○ Central government is not unified but plural; central policies, regulations and incentives are multiple and frequently compete with each other.
○ Central government is fearful of changes that can upset the political process or have an uncontrolled economic impact.

One of the benefits of using a coherent, tested and suitably con-strained operating system is that it enables central policy-makers to become more confident about the possibility of reform and it helps to minimise the risk of unexpected side-effects and the creation of perverse incentives. This means the model is consistent with national policy, but still has the potential to help shift national policy in more helpful directions. Figure 4 sets out this process of double iteration graphically.

The operating system exists in a space between policy-makers and the local champions who must implement policy. As such it enables a

Figure 4 A new operating system

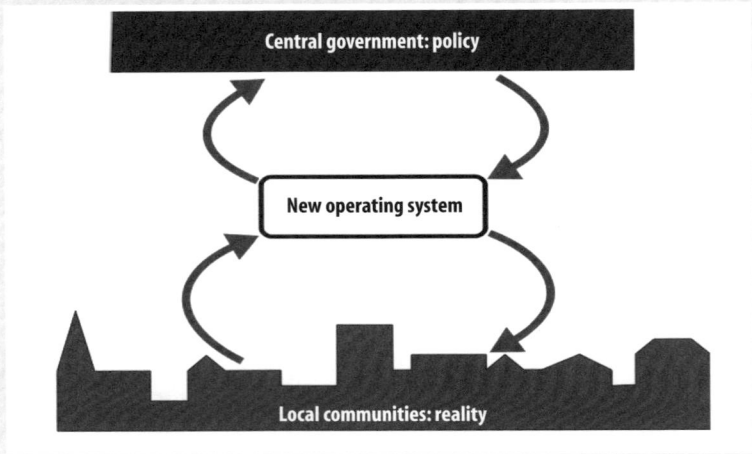

Central government: policy

New operating system

Local communities: reality

Source: in Control

more coherent dialogue between the central and the local; moreover this approach can also foster consensus between those wanting to influence policy. For this reason in Control has found that it has been able to create a coalition of over 20 different partner organisations, ranging from large governmental organisations (like the Care Services Improvement Partnership, CSIP) to small advocacy organisations (like Advocacy Partners). Certainly the impact of in Control's system has now been very significant. Its ideas have been included within several government policies and they are now supported by the Cabinet Office and the Treasury.[10]

Conclusions

Success for in Control is not guaranteed. While there has been a significant level of interest in this approach it is not clear that local or central government will have the will to put in place an extensive programme of systemic change. Social care tends still to be treated as a very marginal part of the welfare system, of interest only to people with the most severe disabilities.

The most hopeful sign is that eight local authorities have come forward to explore what in Control terms total transformation: the development of self-directed support as the only way of providing support. If these authorities prove that the same benefits for disabled people can be achieved for thousands of people, and that this can be done within a sustainable economic framework, then in Control will have helped bring about one of the most important reforms of the welfare state since its inception – a reform that will have been driven by disabled people, families and local communities themselves. All this, from an investment of less than £0.5 million by the Department of Health.

In coming years, the only innovations that will really matter are those that grow out of the intersection between people, their lives and the services they are accessing. Government could learn much from our experience over the last four years about how to invest and support such innovations. Creating more 'in between spaces' for partnerships of users, providers, civil servants and entrepreneurs is a vital ingredient of success. So is the commitment to allow questioning of the 'fundamentals', or the operating systems of services. Had we not questioned the power relationships implicit in current approaches to assessment the in Control model could never have developed an alternative system. Finally, letting us grow, learn and iterate our model without – yet – designing an evaluation that strangles the approach, hints at the need to foster a much stronger culture of learning by doing, rather than implementing or researching impractical or overly abstract policy proposals.

In a world where, as individuals, we expect greater autonomy and freedom, and in a world where demands on the social and health care system are set to grow sharply, it may just be the case that the theme of participation and power become the driving force of innovation. Our politicians and policy-makers need to seize this possibility as their best hope of achieving the kinds of outcomes they are aspiring to.

Simon Duffy is director of in Control.

Notes

1   D Colin-Thomé and G Belfield, *Improving Chronic Disease Management* (London: Department of Health, 2004), available at www.dh.gov.uk/en/ Publicationsandstatistics/Publications/PublicationsPolicyAndGuidance/ DH_4075214 (accessed 13 Apr 2007).

2   See www.in-control.org.uk (accessed 13 Jun 2007).

3   C Poll et al, *A Report on in Control's First Phase 2003–2005* (London: in Control Publications, 2006).

4   See www.individualbudgets.csip.org.uk (accessed 13 Jun 2007).

5   For example in Control has consistently improved its resource allocation system and is currently developing version 5. See S Duffy and J Waters, 'Resource allocation system', discussion paper, Aug 2005, available at www.in-control.org.uk (accessed 13 Jun 2007).

6   For example, people who wish to receive residential care, fully commissioned by the local authority, can still receive this service; however, this must be purchased using their allocation of funding.

7   There are several examples where integrating other funding streams is possible. For example, the Independent Living Fund provides funding for very similar purposes. See M Henwood and B Hudson, *Review of the Independent Living Funds* (London: Department of Work and Pensions, 2007).

8   See S Duffy, 'Economics of self-directed support', discussion paper, Sep 2006, available at www.in-control.org.uk (accessed 13 Jun 2007).

9   The work of in Control has had particular impact on the Cabinet Office's policy document, *Improving the Life Chances of Disabled People* (London: Prime Minister's Strategy Unit, Jan 2005), see www.cabinetoffice.gov.uk/strategy/work_areas/disability/index.asp (accessed 13 Jun 2007).

10 See *Pre-Budget Report 2006* (London: HM Treasury, 2006).

2. Curriculum 2.0

Educating the digital generation*
Keri Facer and Hannah Green

Innovation has been a watchword for educational policy-makers and leading educators in recent years – there have been demands for innovative practice, innovative teachers, innovative leaders. This focus has undoubtedly stimulated some interesting practices and developments. We've seen schools that have challenged standard models of curriculum delivery, opting for condensed four-day timetables or theme-based teaching rather than subject division. We have also seen a proliferation of new models of leadership from individual schools to federations and a shift from centralised to distributed responsibility. These examples of innovation focus on what schools can do to deliver better learning experiences to their students.

However, these models of innovation do not do not address the potential of young people to act as partners in the innovation process. In studying how young people interact with the world around them, it doesn't take long to uncover the fact that any initiative to bring young people into the innovation process will have to grapple with the place of digital technologies in learning as a central element of the

*This paper is based on three research studies: the Demos Digital Curriculum project (2006) run by Hannah Green and Celia Hannon; the ESRC-funded ScreenPlay project run at Bristol University (1998–2001) by John Furlong, Ros Sutherland, Keri Facer and Ruth Furlong; and Keri Facer's PhD research study 'Ideas of childhood and digital technologies in the information age' (2006).

approach. If we are to do justice to the future adults of the twenty-first century, innovation in schools must be driven by young people themselves, and designed from these people outwards, rather than starting with the existing planks of the school system such as the curriculum, pedagogy or buildings.

New skills in the digital age

The employment opportunities awaiting today's young people are changing. Shifts in flows of capital, goods and people, and the emergence of creative and cultural sectors as significant economic forces, mean that states around the world are beginning to re-evaluate the kinds of skills and competencies that people, organisations and institutions need to thrive and flourish in the workplace of the twenty-first century.

Companies in Europe, the US and Japan can produce microchips in Singapore, keypunch data in India, outsource clerical work to Ireland and sell worldwide. From the 1950s onwards jobs in the UK have shifted from production of agricultural and manufactured goods to the production of increasingly sophisticated services and gathering of information. The main ingredient in these services is now knowledge; governments and industry are increasingly asking what the 'new basics' are for the knowledge economy.

This is not merely a concern for the future: many employers are already demanding new skills. While literacy and numeracy are still seen as core requirements, employers are increasingly asking for proof of a range of skills from creativity, ideas generation and presentation, to leadership, team-building and self-confidence. In fact a recent poll of human resources directors showed that employers demand communication skills and think creativity is vital for the future. Importantly for today's pupils, they rated creativity and innovation as the most important graduate skills in ten years' time. We're seeing a shift in demand towards initiative as well as intelligence, creativity as well as qualifications. In other words, we need to see a shift in terms of innovation in schools away from innovative teachers and towards innovative students.

The knowledge economy, then, seems to offer two challenges to formal education: first, it requires a re-evaluation of the skills and competencies required for economic and social survival; second, it requires a re-evaluation of the characteristics and skills which young people themselves may bring into the school system.

The response of formal education

At the present time, the formal education system is struggling to adapt to the changing educational goals and educational subjects of the twenty-first century and to envisage the new institutional, pedagogic and curricular relationships that might be required. While significant progress has been made in raising standards in the 'old basics',[1] progress towards re-imagining educational practices has been fragmented and erratic with only limited connections being made across educational innovation in curriculum, pedagogy and the introduction of digital technologies. In other words, formal education is struggling to meet the challenges of the knowledge economy and the expectations of students who have grown up with the new interactions and practices of the internet.

Attempts by schools to respond to these new demands can be characterised in three primary ways, with many schools working hard to combine elements of all three:

○   From a curricular perspective, a raft of new subjects such as citizenship and enterprise education have found their way onto the curriculum, and work experience is now a statutory part of the Key Stage 4 entitlement. The aim of these new subjects is to foster innovation, creativity and the drive to make things happen.[2] Yet, as Gillinson and O'Leary have pointed out, such an approach suffers from a fundamental problem: it equates the acquisition of skills with specific subjects, and in doing so fails to penetrate vast swathes of the curriculum and compounds the false distinction between knowledge and skills.[3] Alternatives to this approach include the development of competency-

based curricula, such as the RSA's 'Opening Minds'
curriculum which has been adopted enthusiastically by a
large number of schools and the QCA's co-development
networks, which are pioneering programmes of
curriculum and timetable experimentation.

O Another approach, popular among many schools, has
been to shift attention away from a concern with
curriculum to an emphasis on pedagogic innovation. This
has led to experimentation with new teaching techniques
aimed at fostering 'learning to learn', 'thinking skills' and
'assessment for learning',[4] which are believed to encourage
increased learner agency and responsibility for learning,
and hence to foster the development of new skills.

O A further response to addressing the new demands of the
knowledge economy has been a significant and impressive
investment in school hardware and software. Secondary
schools now spend £91 per pupil per year on information
and communication technology (ICT), the government
has promised another £1.7 billion by 2008,[5] and the
development of ICT skills is now a core entitlement of the
UK national curriculum.

Much has been written elsewhere about the first two of these
approaches; this essay is primarily concerned with the third. Without
a deeper understanding of how technology can aid new educational
goals and pedagogies, this investment in new equipment will remain
under-exploited. ICT in schools is predicated on the 'top-down'
understanding that we know how children should be learning from
technology rather than seeking to learn from their existing practices.

Rather than harnessing the technologies that are already fully
integrated into young people's daily lives, schools (and many of the
technical systems they have bought into) primarily have a 'battening
down the hatches' approach. Responding to concerns about the safety
of social networking sites, most schools block MySpace, YouTube and
Bebo. Mobiles, iPods and other pieces of equipment are similarly

unwelcome in the classroom. Meanwhile, teachers often do not feel confident using hardware or software – many know less than their students. Unless they follow their own enthusiasm, they are unlikely to have the skills – teacher training requires only basic competency in email, Word and Excel.

A generation of 'digital natives'

Study of how young people use and relate to technology in their lives is instructive. For nearly a quarter of a century[6] researchers have been arguing that young people's use of digital technologies outside school equip them better for the twenty-first century than their experiences at school. Advocates of computer games have been particularly vocal in this respect, arguing, for example, that

> *Video games are perfect training for life [...] where daily existence demands the ability to parse 16 kinds of information being fired at you simultaneously from telephones, televisions, fax machines, pagers, personal digital assistants, voice messaging systems, postal delivery, e-mail and the internet.*[7]

More recently, research into online environments – such as collaborative knowledge production sites like Wikipedia, or massive multiplayer online games like Everquest – suggests that young people who use these tools are developing skills of information analysis, knowledge production, team working and so forth. With the advent of blogging and other social software tools, researchers are seeing the development of new identities for young people, who are just as likely to seek feedback from their peers and strangers as they are from teachers and parents. This has led to a blurring of the boundaries between expert and amateur, friend and mentor.

Online games environments, some argue, are powerful learning communities that encourage the development of a range of skills such as attracting, evaluating and recruiting new members; creating apprenticeship programmes; orchestrating group strategy; and managing disputes. Sonia Livingstone characterises it in terms of a broader societal shift: 'a blurring of key boundaries between producers and consumers, work and leisure, entertainment and information'.[8] These academic arguments are echoed by leading-edge tech companies that are developing alternative recruitment methods and appealing for people with skills developed in online and games environments.[9]

These arguments are best summed up in the concept of the 'digital native', which presents a view of young people born after the mid-1970s as an entirely new 'digital generation' with the skills to cope with the challenges of the knowledge economy more effectively than adults:

In today's world most adults would do very badly as kids. There are many more complexities, ambiguities and differences . . . because we have an information access which reaches across the planet. . . . Kids can empower themselves and see new notions of work and play, society and self, teaching and learning – concepts which no longer have these crisp lines separating one from the other.[10]

The twenty-first century as a post-school era?

Does this matter? If young people are developing the skills and competencies to navigate the information society successfully through playing computer games, why should schools change their curriculum or pedagogy? One model of change that could be imagined from this argument is that schools wither away as young people increasingly learn through networks, drawing on personal and domestic digital technologies as sources of learning and ways of connecting with others.

The concept of being able to get access to information outside the school walls has seen some commentators promote home-schooling and online learning as a viable and desirable alternative or addition to the state system. Similarly, even for those who do not herald the end of schools as we know them in the digital era, there is a view that schools do not need to respond to these new patterns of learning and interaction beyond the school gate, and should focus instead on the more traditional dimensions of the curriculum.

We find such arguments problematic. Our research has demonstrated time and again that a formal education system that fails to engage with young people on their terms risks turning our children off learning for life. Equally significantly, the problem with these arguments is that they suppose that digital skills are innate – that 'digital natives' emerge fully formed and information literate from the womb. As Sefton-Green argues:

> *There seems to be a political consensus that the school cannot be the sole resource for educating a future society, but the answer to this problem seems to be that middle-class parents supplement state schooling in their information-rich homes – barely an equitable solution . . . and embracing this position merely serves (yet again) to discriminate in favour of the middle class.*[11]

Indeed, arguments which suggest that young people will inevitably, and naturally, develop 'knowledge economy skills' by virtue of access to digital technologies outside school are fundamentally divorced from an understanding of the material conditions within which children are enabled to develop these skills. Such arguments are, typically, blind to the resources (financial, cultural and material) that enable the development of such skills. They overlook the extent to which access to and use of digital technologies is predicated on domestic access to internet connections and to participation in family cultures which encourage exploration and play with digital environments. A supportive family environment means that children can get advice when they become stuck, and that they have access to the cultural and financial resources to create new and more stretching challenges. Such arguments also, moreover, overlook the extent to which the development of 'knowledge economy' skills are produced in cultural contexts.

If we consider, for example, two different accounts of children's computer use presented in a study of domestic technologies,[12] we see two very different views of the interactions and competencies developed in using digital technologies. Mrs Smith (left school at 14, works in the home bringing up five children and makes no use of the home computer) described the reason for her children using computers as follows:

> *I think that's good, it's good. Plus as you know everything's computers nowadays. Office, computer, everything is ... the file bit is gone now, everything is just done on the computer, your records, everything. So I think it's because the more they learn the more experience they have. Offices, everything is just computers.*

Mr Grant (educated to degree level, a strategic analyst for a major international corporation, who runs the home computer and manages it for the family) described his sons' interaction with computers as follows:

> *I think another important skill is being able to figure things out relatively quickly as well, you know ... so even if they're just playing games and figuring things out for themselves I think the confidence to do it and then the sort of ability to just play with things until they get it right is very important ... there's playing with it in such a way that actually gets to the end point that you want, that's the key thing you know.*

It is worth comparing these accounts with the predictions of Manuel Castells (author of *The Rise of the Network Society*) who argued that the knowledge economy would witness the development of two types of workers – self-generative workers and generic workers. The self-generative workers would be:

> *able constantly to redefine the necessary skills for a given task, and to access the sources for learning these skills*[13]

and 'generic workers' would be:

> 'human terminals' [who] can, of course, be replaced by machines, or by any other body around the city, the country or the world, depending on business decisions. While they are collectively indispensable to the production process, they are individually expendable.[14]

When we compare Mr Grants's language of performance monitoring, progression, play and self-analysis with Mrs Smith's language of experience of office skills, it seems likely that a formal education system which fails to develop an interconnected innovation strategy across curricula, pedagogy and digital technologies will guarantee that some children rather than others are predisposed to succeed or fail in the competitive environment of the twenty-first century.

Recommendations

Transformation in school practices is required as a matter of urgency in order to maintain the role and function of schools as valuable and valid resources for all children in the country. The failure to ensure integrated innovation of pedagogy, curriculum and institutions will see increasing numbers of children and families leave the state system to explore home, personal and online learning approaches, and will see other children receiving a 'basic' education, which will provide little compensation for lack of material, cultural and financial resources outside the school.

This essay has argued that such a transformation needs to grow out of a deeper understanding of the lives and behaviours and learning styles of young people. In these terms, the change needed in schools is threefold.

First, schools need to find ways to understand, recognise and value the learning that goes on outside the classroom.

Second, schools need to support this learning, to galvanise and develop it so students can recognise and transfer those skills in new situations and contexts.

Finally, and critically, schools need to understand the resources that go into enabling such learning and find ways of making them visible within the formal education system. They need to work with 'digital natives' to understand the means by which such competencies are developed. For example, this could be about giving young people control of a creative portfolio that enables them to capture and share achievements from different spheres of their lives, introducing peer-to-peer technology tuition to build on the way we know young people are learning, or setting up class wikis to develop skills around collaboration and teamwork that are second nature for young people playing online games.

Digital natives are bred not born; competence is created through interactions and resources and time, not innate in a particular generation. We need to better understand the means by which such competencies are built and work with young people to generate new strategies for teaching and learning in state education, which ensures that all young people, not just the early adopters and enthusiasts, are supported to develop these competencies. We must stop treating young people as empty vessels to be filled and begin to see them as vital and valuable resources in their own right.

We might also want to question the assumption that raising standards in 'the basics' is an effective strategy for achieving social justice in the context of a new knowledge economy. Does this emphasis guarantee that formal state education focuses on the lowest common denominator skills while ensuring that middle-class households are able to develop 'information age skills' in the home? If we start from an interest in enabling all young people to live and succeed in the complex spaces of the knowledge economy, we need to make sure that experiences such as collaborative learning, personal development, self-monitoring, 'creativity' and 'thinking' skills are developed as a matter of course in schools.

These competencies will need to be nurtured through both curricular and pedagogic reform. Many educators have resisted the concept of formally assessing 'soft skills' such as creativity and thinking skills, yet the failure to explicitly articulate what these skills might look like, how they might be exemplified, and how progression and development might be considered could be seen to privilege those who are already familiar with and equipped to develop such skills:

> *When the 'rules of the game' and the forms of language that society rewards are left implicit, to be discovered (inferred) by students as they are immersed in meaningful activities, we simply privilege children from families where these 'rules' and forms are already part of their social practices.*[15]

We need to create bridges between what pupils are learning in school and what they are learning out of school, but it would be a mistake to assume that we can do this by absorbing informal learning into the classroom. Instead, we need adults to understand the valuable aspects of informal learning, to isolate those positives and to help develop them further in a school environment.

In short, young people must be seen as partners in future educational innovation, if we are to be sure that such processes do not just produce more of the same, but instead more of what is needed. Only through starting with young people and how they relate to the world around them can we begin to build a strategic idea of the new role of teachers and other adults in formal education. Where some are scared of losing adult authority in the light of some children's capacities with digital technologies, the shift to the knowledge economy, and its implications for adulthood for today's young people, makes this focus imperative. It is the *only* way that we can renew our confidence in what it is that adults and schools can offer children in the midst of the complexities, delights and desires of the information age.

Keri Facer is the research director at Future Lab and Hannah Green is a senior researcher at Demos.

Notes

1   The number of students achieving level 5 at Key Stage 2 SATS has grown from 14% in 1995 to 37% by 2006 and the number achieving a level 4 has risen by 47%, from 55% to 81%. The number of students achieving five A*–C (including English and Maths) at GCSE has also increased, from 35.2% in 1996 to 44.9% in 2005. See www.dfes.gov.uk/rsgateway/DB/VOL/v000063/se2-t9a.htm (accessed 12 Dec 2006).

2   Government response to Paul Robert's *Report on Nurturing Creativity in Young People* (London: Department for Culture, Media and Sport, 2006).

3   S Gillinson and D O'Leary, *Working Progress: How to reconnect young people and organisations* (London: Demos, 2006).

4   G Claxton, *Building Learning Power: Helping young people to become better learners* (Bristol: TLO, 2002); P Black and D Williams, *Inside the Black Box: Raising standards through classroom assessment* (London: Kings College, 1998).

5   See http://news.bbc.co.uk/1/hi/education/4161233.stm (accessed 24 Jun 2007).

6   See, for example, SS Baugham and PD Clagett, *Video Games and Human Development: A research agenda for the 80s* (Cambridge, MA: Harvard Graduate School of Education, 1983); S Papert, *Mindstorms: Children, computers and powerful ideas*, 2nd edn (New York: Perseus Books, 1993).

7   JC Herz, *Joystick Nation* (Boston: Little, Brown, 1997).

8   S Livingstone and M Bovill, *Young People, New Media*, final report of the project 'Children, young people and the changing media environment', an LSE report (London: London School of Economics, 1999).

9   J Seely Brown and D Thomas, '"You play World of Warcraft? You're hired!" Why multiplayer games may be the best kind of job training', *Wired*, 14 Apr 2006.

10 N Negroponte, 'Foreword' in S Papert, *The Connected Family: Bridging the digital generation gap* (Atlanta, GA: Longstreet Press, 1996).

11 J Sefton-Green (ed), *Digital Diversions: Youth culture in the age of multimedia* (London: University College London, 1998).

12 From K Facer et al, *ScreenPlay: Children's use of computers in the home* (London: Routledge, 2003).

13 M Castells, *The Rise of the Network Society (The Information Age: Economy, society and culture: Vol 1)* (Boston and Oxford: Blackwell Publishers, 1996).

14 M Castells, *The End of Millenium (The Information Age: Economy, society and culture: Vol 3)* (Boston and Oxford: Blackwell Publishers, 1997).

15 J Gee, G Hull and C Lankshear, *The New Work Order: Behind the language of new capitalism* (St Leonards, NSW: Allen and Unwin, 1996).

3. Doctor, the patient will see you now

Participating and innovating in healthcare

Jack Stilgoe and Faizal Farook

If one asks lawyers, architects, social workers, or management consultants whether they prefer clients who take an interest in the issues they face and are motivated to work in partnership to achieve successful results, the answer seems obvious. So why does the idea of expert patients provoke such antipathy within the medical profession?

Editorial, *British Medical Journal*, 27 March 2004

In healthcare, change is irresistible. New and increasingly expensive technologies and techniques constantly offer solutions to health problems, helping to create continually rising expectations and demands from politicians, patients and the public. As old problems are solved, new ones are created. The energy of the twentieth-century NHS was spent on the treatment of acute illness and injury. But the answers the service found to that challenge simply begged further questions. As healthcare institutions became more effective at prolonging life, they had to learn to deal with increasing levels of long-term illness. As basic healthcare needs were met, they were replaced by a nebulous set of less-understood lifestyle illnesses.

In 2002 the Wanless Review delivered a stark message to the Treasury.[1] On current trends, by 2022, health spending could double to 12.5 per cent of GDP. A huge proportion of the pressure for this increase would come from chronic conditions like diabetes. After decades of underinvestment, the NHS needed significantly more investment to catch up with current demand, and then to change its practices radically to meet current and future challenges. Wanless offered a Hobson's choice of three models, with the clear implication that a sustainable NHS would have to be 'fully engaged' – with people taking a direct role in co-producing their own health. An innovative NHS therefore needed to find new ways of getting people involved.

But with all the effort expended on a particular kind of 'modernisation' of the health service over the past decade, it is notable that most of the innovation has focused on new technology and management systems. The everyday conversations between healthcare professionals and the people they serve have been relatively neglected, despite the fact that these conversations are where government policy, new technology and patient needs meet. Conversation is the first step in any episode of healthcare, allowing patients to set the context for everything that follows. It shapes and defines the healthcare need, allowing professional and patient to identify the problem effectively before seeking solutions via co-production, participation and a choice of providers.

Improving the quality of the conversations between patient and professional is a vital part of any attempt to create a sustainable NHS, but the innovations necessary to make this happen will involve changing people's tacit and intuitive behaviour. This kind of change is inherently difficult for central policy-makers to understand or control. It involves fundamentally reassessing what patients want from professionals and taking a fresh look at the skills required by professionals themselves.

The new paternalism

Current health reforms acknowledge that greater participation by service users is vital, but the nature of this participation and its links to innovation are still being negotiated. Arguments about patient and public involvement, contestability or choice all reflect particular views of the desires and roles of professionals, patients and citizens.[2] The current prevailing wisdom is that people should be given 'a stronger voice so that they are the major drivers of service improvement'.[3]

But while people are imagined as consumers sending signals to the health service through their choices, they are seldom seen as having much of a role to play once their choice has been made. Their role as dispensers of voice, choice and exit is central, while their everyday experiences at hospitals, GPs' surgeries and elsewhere are overlooked.

Current reforms see greater engagement as a way of delivering services more efficiently, rather than questioning the basis and the limits of the services being provided. Harry Cayton, the government's patient tsar, underlines the point when he argues that services are still run mostly in the interests of producers, not through malice, but because the interests of service users are more often assumed than explored.[4] This model of healthcare and its implementation is still overwhelmingly paternalistic. Patients are still largely seen as passive and inexpert recipients of professional expertise. They are consumers, not contributors.

Innovation for healthcare needs to resist the managerial temptation to limit the space for participation. Instead, an innovative health service needs to allow its users to define the terms of participation. As our opening quote identifies, in some professional areas this message is an easy one to transmit. In healthcare, it requires asking some fundamental questions about professional culture. We need to go beyond the everyday paternalism that still defines the relationship between doctor and patient, between the NHS and its public.

The fully engaged NHS demanded by Wanless requires a professional culture to match the new context of health and illness and the new context of public expectation. According to one recent study, the UK is falling behind in its attempts to keep pace with the need for engaged healthcare.[5]

However, the challenges of the future also contain the seeds of the solution. A re-negotiation of participation is already happening, bringing new, unacknowledged drivers for innovation. Whether professionals enjoy them or not, new conversations are already taking place that question the old distinctions between professional and public, expert and user. GPs throughout the UK are now faced with patients who, with easy access to a wealth of information and support online, are ready to play a more assertive role in the definition of their illness and the identification of treatments and preventative measures.[6]

These people are not *consumers* of the service, helping to deliver what the NHS wants to give them, nor are they simply *designers* of the service. They are one half of the conversation that determines their own health. Inevitably, there is still a huge asymmetry of expertise. But the questions they ask of the NHS can no longer be ignored.

At the least, they are indicative of a public desire to play a role that is markedly different from that traditionally imagined by industrial medicine. These new conversations are still in their infancy, and the reaction to them is still mainly defensive – patients carrying pages from the internet are sometimes referred to as suffering from 'cyberchondria'.[7] But we have started to see examples of innovations that tap the resource of entrepreneurial patients and demonstrate change – beyond efficiency and beyond participation, to a richer sense of engagement with healthcare.

Case 1: The Evelina Children's Hospital

It is safe to say that there is no other hospital in the world where you will find Spiderman cleaning the windows. But it is not just for this reason that the Evelina Children's Hospital stands out as an example of the type of innovation the NHS can produce at its best. Using money from their charity fund and public donors, Guy's and St Thomas' set out to create a 'hospital that doesn't feel like a hospital'. The hospital was built on the understanding that child patients' and families' experiences were not incidental to treatment but an integral part of the healing process. A giant glass atrium that blurs the boundary between the hospital and the neighbouring park, a school for long-term patients, fold-down beds in every room for parents to sleep over, 'wiggly' wards that intimidate children less than long straight ones, and window cleaners dressed as superheroes are just some of its unique features.

We did not just offer service users a limited consultation process, but made them part of the design process. The trust uniquely created a Children's Board, consisting of child patients, their families and local school children, which was involved throughout on design and operational issues, influencing everything from the design of the building down to even the hospital menus.

The innovative approach at Evelina has spread beyond hospital design – the hospital brought in actors to convey scenarios based on patients' stories, helping to implement ground-breaking staff training. Doctors and nurses embrace change readily and staff recruitment focuses on recruiting staff with not just technical skills but the personal attributes to ensure a positive experience for patients and their families.

Case 2: Expert patients

As many as 17 million adults in the UK may be living with a long-term health condition. In 2002 the government began piloting its Expert Patients Programme (EPP), in which such patients are invited to join groups that provide support and information. This programme was prompted by a realisation that in most cases of chronic illness, healthcare is as much about monitoring as it is about treatment. The programme helps to share responsibility for healthcare between patients and the NHS, build trust in the information they are accessing and help patients to learn together about how best to cope with their conditions. Helped by trained volunteers with similar conditions, patients learn more about how to manage their illness.

According to a recent pilot evaluation, 45 per cent of EPP participants said that they felt more confident that common symptoms would no longer interfere with their lives, 38 per cent felt that such symptoms were less severe four to six months after completing the course, and 33 per cent felt better prepared for consultations with health professionals. The reduced burden on normal services was also clear (7 per cent reductions in GP consultations, 10 per cent reductions in outpatient visits, 16 per cent reductions in Accident & Emergency attendances and 9 per cent reductions in physiotherapy use).[8]

The EPP recognises that knowledge can empower people. But the first phases of the programme have tried to keep control of what patients know about their illness. Through the courses that make up the programme, knowledge is translated downwards to patients. Less recognition is given either to what patients already know about their illness or to how patients can help build collective knowledge themselves. The EPP, as it was originally conceived, is missing out on a huge potential resource. One respondent to the *BMJ* editorial quoted at the top of this chapter reflects a widely held feeling:

> *I'm guilty! Since being diagnosed with sarcoidosis, I've turned into one of those dreaded internet-scouring patients who present their docs with a sheaf of downloaded research papers . . . call me a fellow researcher, if you will, with a particularly strong motivation to succeed at the job. . . . There is only one medical thing I'm an expert in, and that's how my condition affects me. . . . So I appeal to all you medics: stay humble, stay alert to new research, even if it is presented to you by an unskilled, untrained, common-or-garden patient!*[9]

That the EPP had to defend itself as 'not an anti-professional initiative'[10] reminds us of the context in which it operates. It is easy for professionals to see such innovations as yet another source of pressure. But expertise is not a zero-sum game. Empowering patients does not mean that the knowledge of professionals is being challenged. It does mean that professionals have to renegotiate their role, to move beyond expertise as *knowledge* to a model of expertise as *wisdom*.[11]

The EPP is now rolling out to the NHS in general, and has become a community interest company, giving it space to develop a richer, more productive conversation between patients and professionals.[12] It is now up to core services to use the EPP in the most productive way possible.

Case 3: Patient opinion

Patient Opinion (www.patientopinion.org.uk) is a social enterprise that looks to tap into bottom-up public and patient conversation about health services. It provides a forum for public expression, linked to hospitals and trusts. The space it provides is open, allowing people to define their own response to services in rich, multi-dimensional narratives. The website lets people themselves define their own interaction with their health service. The stories are about quality and efficiency of treatment, but they also talk about management, dignity and the quality of conversation that takes place as services are provided.

NHS managers are starting to sign up to the service. The stories are peppered with ideas for service improvement, but managers will need to learn how to listen to them. One thing is certain: the sort of discussion that Patient Opinion reveals will not go away. Indeed Paul Hodgkin, a GP and founder of Patient Opinion, points to new ways in which discussions will become visible and increasingly uncomfortable. How will an NHS trust react when photos of its hospital toilets are uploaded to Flickr? Whether this is seen as a resource or a threat is a question of professional practice and culture.[13]

Conclusion

The future evolution and survival of the NHS depends ultimately on a culture shift within the service: from seeing the patient not as part of a problem but as part of the solution to their own healthcare needs.

Health professionals are used to a paternalistic relationship due to historically large asymmetries of information between them and their patients. But at the start of the twenty-first century the information exchange is more complicated. Education levels are higher and access to relevant medical information online means that patients can contribute to understanding and making sense of their symptoms. As a result, in line with wider cultural shifts, patients want and expect more say in their healthcare. This change is unavoidable, but it contains the seeds for future NHS innovation and improvement.

Traditionally the medical community has been antipathetic to active, involved patients, seeing them as an inconvenience rather than a potential partner. Questioning patients are more effort-intensive than passive ones, and real conversation uses up valuable clinical time. As such the system is configured in a way that patients are given a selection of pre-defined responses and interactions rather than the opportunity to define and shape the conversation about their health on their own terms.

By allowing people more control over their treatment (and giving them more responsibility for it) we can achieve outcomes that suit patients better and create a more efficient system. Although reshaping the doctor–patient relationship into a more cooperative partnership will require more face-to-face time spent educating and explaining, this actually creates greater capacity in the long term by enabling patients to self-manage treatments and procedures that would otherwise require NHS resources.

Policy areas that hinge on expertise carry an unresolved tension – between participation and standardisation. Recent years have seen moves towards greater engagement in health policy, but there has also been a growing emphasis on standardisation and spreading best practice, under the banner of evidence-based medicine. Though this seems like a straightforwardly sensible idea, in practice it can create a high-minded professionalism that narrows the space for patient questions, professional judgement and innovation. Encouraging change in health services means appreciating some of the limits of evidence-based rhetoric and allowing a more open space for conversation.

Changing the relationship with health professionals does not invalidate or diminish the need for professional judgement and expertise. Patients will always require the clinical knowledge and insight of professionals – skills that cannot be fully replicated by the internet. Indeed, some of the tools that empower patients may also contain threats to their wellbeing. Recent research found that people searching online for health advice favoured sources that featured personal testimonies from like-minded peers rather than those with the highest-quality information, such as NHS direct.[14] In the future, doctors will need to acknowledge that their authority will derive more and more from a position of trusted guide and partner, rather than as an encyclopaedia of medical information.

Health professionals already have the skills to deliver a more engaged kind of healthcare – all they require is a shift in emphasis. Successful patient conversation will depend on high-calibre interpersonal skills underpinned by faith in patients' judgements and abilities. But conversation also takes time and energy, which means that professionals need to be given the space and resources necessary without patient contact time being restricted by narrow performance measures and underfunding.

As our case studies highlight, engaged, empowered patients can improve their own outcomes, raise those of other patients and help to create a more effective healthcare system overall. Evelina Hospital demonstrates how patients moving beyond consultation to co-production can create a higher-quality, more innovative and more effective service. And this does not have to mean more expensive. The final cost of the Evelina Hospital was £60 million, the same per square foot as a regular PFI (private finance initiative) build.[15]

Early evidence from the Expert Patient Programme shows that 'peer-to-peer' learning, if utilised appropriately, can improve patient outcomes and concomitantly reduce the need to access health services. As Patient Opinion expands, it will provide countless recipes for service improvement and hints for innovation.

To date, the focus of much NHS reform has been on increasing the efficiency of existing ways of working, to raise the baseline of healthcare provision to a satisfactory level. Now that this has been achieved, however, it is not enough for our health service to simply carry on doing the same things in a more efficient manner. The case studies we cite demonstrate how the NHS can, and must, move to a new, more collaborative, patient-centred model of care to remain effective, not merely efficient.

It is through harnessing the ability and energy of the patient that we will shape and create an NHS fit for the future. Involved, engaged patients can make decisions on their care based on their needs rather than those of the system. Technological and cultural changes will allow these same patients to become responsible for more elements of their treatment, thus reducing reliance on the NHS. Using these developments will be a vital part in reshaping the NHS as a preventative rather than reactive healthcare system, and as a democratic rather than plutocratic entity.

Jack Stilgoe is a senior researcher and Faizal Farook is a researcher at Demos.

Notes

1   D Wanless, *Securing our Future Health: Taking a long-term view* (London: HM Treasury, 2002), available at www.hm-treasury.gov.uk/consultations_and_legislation/wanless/consult_wanless_final.cfm (accessed 11 Apr 2007).

2   See E Andersson, J Tritter and R Wilson (eds), *Healthy Democracy: The future of involvement in health and social care* (London: Involve, 2006).

3   DoH, *Our Health, Our Care, Our Say: A new direction for community services* (London: Department of Health, 2006).

4   See H Cayton, 'Patients as entrepreneurs; who is in charge of change?' in Andersson et al, *Healthy Democracy*.

5   A Coulter, *Engaging Patients in their Healthcare: How is the UK doing relative to other countries?* (Oxford: Picker Institute Europe, 2006).

6   J Stilgoe, A Irwin and K Jones, *The Received Wisdom: Opening up expert advice* (London: Demos, 2006).

7   JA Fowell, M Darvell and JAM Gray, 'The doctor, the patient and the world-wide web: how the internet is changing healthcare', *Journal of the Royal Society of Medicine* 96, no 2 (Feb 2003).

8   NHS, 'Stepping stones to success: an implementation, training and support framework for lay led self-management', 2005, www.expertpatients.nhs.uk/public/default.aspx?load=ArticleViewer&ArticleId=445 (accessed 14 Jun 2007).

9   Response to editorial '"Expert patient": dream or nightmare?', *bmj.com*, 1 Apr 2004, see www.bmj.com/cgi/eletters/328/7442/723#55187 (accessed 14 Jun 2007).

10 DoH, *The Expert Patient: A new approach to chronic disease management for the 21st century* (London: Department of Health, 2001).

11   Stilgoe et al, *Received Wisdom*.

12   E Miliband MP, speech at an event to celebrate first anniversary of Community Interest Companies, London, 10 Jul 2006.

13   See www.patientopinion.org.uk (accessed 14 Jun 2007) and 'Voice of opinions', *SocietyGuardian*, 28 Feb 2007.

14   E Sillence, P Briggs and A Herxheimer, 'Personal experiences matter: what patients think about hypertension information online', *Health Information on the Internet*, 42 (Dec 2004).

15   H Pearman, 'Just what the doctor ordered', *Sunday Times*, 27 Nov 2005.

Localities

4. Localism and innovation

A driver for innovation?
Paul Coen and Matthew Warburton

Local government is no stranger to innovation. The high Victorian glory days of municipal government are famous for the variety and importance of the public service innovations to which they gave birth – clean water, sewerage, town gas, electricity, street lighting, public parks, hospitals, schools and council housing. This capacity did not disappear with top hats and steam power. The last four decades offer numerous examples of locally initiated innovation, including local economic development work, new approaches to tackling racial inequality, partnerships with the voluntary sector and experiments with neighbourhood devolution.

Local government's strength as an innovator lies in its decentralisation and diversity. With 420 councils in England and Wales tackling local variations of broadly similar problems, it is hardly surprising that there is a constant stream of new ideas being converted into innovative practice in individual councils – and not just those labelled 'excellent'. But local government's strength is also its weakness; despite all the ideas being generated, councils have not been good enough at sharing and learning from each other. That is why bringing innovation to scale across local government is the key challenge for the sector.

Just as it is possible to point to shining examples of innovative policies and practices in some councils, it is possible to find councils which seem averse to change and blind to urgent local challenges.

Advocates of localism tend to focus on the former, while central government's concern has more often been with the latter. The overall result is a familiar pattern of reform in which local initiatives from the best councils have often been followed up by legislation to ensure national take-up. Services that were once provided locally in some parts of the country become nationalised (and sometimes later privatised) to ensure national coverage to minimum standards. From water, gas and electricity to universal education and council housing, municipal innovations have always fed national reform programmes.

So the centralising urge of the last decade is not a new feature of national government. It is the chosen instruments of centralisation that are different. The Blair government has been more reluctant than some of its predecessors to remove functions from councils. Its distinctive creation has been the plethora of statutory plans, indicators, targets, standards and specific funding arrangements to which councils are expected to conform. These arrangements have placed new and tighter limits on local government's difference and distinctiveness, and hence on the sector's inherent ability to innovate.

The greatest opportunity for a generation

The 2006 local government white paper[1] marks the government's acknowledgement of the need to move on to a more decentralised and devolved system that gives councils and local service partners more freedom to respond to local needs and wishes. It reflects a recognition across government, growing for some time, that the centralist approach cannot hope to meet the challenges facing public services as we go into the twenty-first century. People and places are becoming more diverse. Service users increasingly have distinctive individual needs and wishes, as well as higher expectations that services will be tailored to meet them. Neighbourhoods, towns and cities are also becoming more diverse and need to pursue their own distinctive roads to prosperity and success.

For the next decade at least, the response to these challenges must be delivered within tight financial limits since significant increases in overall taxation are not an option. This creates very substantial pressure to contain costs and improve efficiency. A third consideration is that many of the more intractable problems facing government, nationally and locally, demand better coordination of local responses between councils and a variety of other service providers, which cannot be orchestrated from Whitehall.

In this context, there is little option for government but to decentralise and deregulate. Only by bringing key decisions closer to the user and citizen is it possible to make policies and services more responsive to individual and local needs and wishes. Giving partnerships of local service providers wider freedom to reconfigure services makes it possible both to provide better access and choice, and to improve efficiency by reducing duplication and achieving economies of scale.

It is important not to underestimate the cultural barriers to achieving greater localism – while ministers and civil servants recognise the case intellectually, it will not be easy for them to actually relinquish the centralist habits of a lifetime. But the white paper nonetheless presents councils with their greatest opportunity and greatest challenge for a generation. For the first time in two decades, what happens next is really up to local government, rather than ministers and civil servants.

The latest Comprehensive Performance Assessment (CPA) results show that four councils out of five are performing well and continuing to improve, in some cases strongly. Their record on efficiency leads the public sector. But councils face a cultural challenge at least as great as that confronting Whitehall. It has been said, with some truth, that the great strength of councils has been their ability to handle whatever the government has thrown at them. The down side, however, is that the habits of reaction and compliance may have become deeply ingrained. Symptoms include a narrow interpretation of council powers and freedoms, and dependence on government guidance in responding to new legislation and new challenges.

Councils now need to develop new strengths – to innovate in response to changing needs and priorities, to take the lead in setting clear ambitions for their communities and working with others to deliver them, rather than waiting for initiatives from Whitehall. This brings the original challenge to the sector back into sharp relief: if innovation cannot be driven from the centre then what else can be done, in the locality as much as from the centre, to foster and promote local government innovation?

Fostering innovation

Much attention has been focused over the last decade on the challenge of local government improvement. Our key conclusion from this experience is that improvement is inextricably linked to a council's capacity to innovate, and that innovation by definition comes from within organisations – it cannot be imposed from without.

This model of councils driving improvement for themselves sharply contradicts the common assumption that there is a single, detailed model of best practice for a local government service that can be taken up from leading-edge organisations and implemented across the sector as a whole. In this superficially compelling model, the instruments of policy are legislation, statutory guidance, inspection and peer pressure. This is, of course, a caricature, exaggerated to make a point. But it is not far from the assumptions underlying much recent public policy on improvement.

The reason that this model does not hold true is simple – no hard line can be drawn between coming up with a new idea and implementing practice from elsewhere. Putting a new idea into operation, even if that idea comes from a neighbouring local authority, must always involve an element of innovation. The new idea has to be interpreted and tailored in the context of distinctive local processes and culture, and the service itself must be adapted to local needs and circumstances. One size really does not fit all.

It follows that the key to fostering innovation is fostering the capacity of every council to innovate for itself. How can we recognise councils that have this capacity? A literature review commissioned by the Local Government Association (LGA) from the Tavistock

Institute suggests that the following key factors are likely to characterise public service organisations capable of innovation:

○   an innovative culture supported from the top of the organisation, including appropriate incentives and rewards for innovation
○   the ability to listen to and learn from service users, staff and other stakeholders; diversity of staff and users is a benefit because it provides a range of different perspectives
○   a habit of 'getting out' to look at and learn from other organisations tackling similar problems
○   the ability to contain short-term pressures and priorities, take the longer view and create the time and 'safe spaces' in which innovation can be nurtured and tested
○   the capacity to manage risk, rather than being adverse to it.

Conversely, the barriers to innovation include:

○   delivery pressures and administrative burdens that deny staff time to think about doing things differently
○   short-term budgets and planning horizons
○   poor rewards and incentives to innovate
○   a culture of risk aversion and poor skills in active risk or change management.

This analysis will chime immediately with anyone familiar with local government's experience over the last decade, and in particular the developing story of Local Public Service Agreements (LPSAs) and Local Area Agreements (LAAs) – a new approach to central/local relations that is slowly trying to replace prescription and legislation with individual negotiation about a local authority's goals.

In 1998, the LGA published *The Local Challenge*,[2] which called on the government to test a new way of linking national objectives with local needs and circumstances. Councils would commit with local partners to deliver better outcomes on key government ambitions such as crime reduction, getting people into work or raising educational standards. In return they would receive freedom from legislative burdens that obstructed innovation and diverted attention from delivery.

From 1999 this proposal was rolled out across local government in the form of LPSAs, which included the added incentive of financial assistance to pump-prime innovation and financial rewards for successful delivery of agreed targets. A second, more ambitious, generation of central–local agreements followed from 2003. LAAs were a natural development, widening the scope of the agreements and providing greater freedom to deploy area-based funding streams. Encouraged by the LGA in our 2006 manifesto *Closer to People and Places*,[3] the government proposed to make second-generation LAAs the key mechanism through which its promise to decentralise would be delivered, and the centrepiece of a future performance framework for local public services. It is therefore enormously important that they succeed.

On the surface, this story might appear to be one of steady progress from silo-driven centralism towards the vision first set out in *The Local Challenge*. Looking deeper, however, it is clear that part of the original vision has been lost. Pioneers of LPSAs recall with some nostalgia how once having agreed their set of 'stretched' performance targets, they had three years to deliver on them. In some cases they delivered in two years or even less, but the important point was that they were given the space and time to design, nurture and test new and more effective ways of delivering services or achieving outcomes. The current LAA regime, with its over-reliance on indicators, targets and close performance monitoring, tends to deny councils the space to innovate and to reward compliance over innovation. It is essential that in the design of the next generation of LAAs we return to that original vision of a focus on delivery, ambition and innovation.

But there are lessons for local government, too. The success of LPSAs lay in the opportunity and 'permission' given to councils, with their partners, to challenge established practice, think unthinkable thoughts and find new ways of doing things. The 'freedoms and flexibilities' granted through the process were less important, the search for them often proving frustrating and fruitless. Central government proved unwilling to grant significant freedoms if they were seen to compromise key policies or priorities. But councils often asked for freedoms which, on a close examination of the law, they already had. In many cases, the barriers to innovation were not legal but lay more in the established mindset and culture of councils and their partners.

Raising our game

To rise to the challenges of the twenty-first century, local government has to learn how to raise its game through its own initiative and efforts. It needs to be capable of improving without the spur – often misdirected – of government intervention. The key to this is about individual councils, with their partners, learning how to welcome and respond to the spur of local needs and wishes, using them as a stimulus for improving the lives of local people and their satisfaction with local public services.

But an equally important requirement is for the local government sector as a whole to respond to the challenge posed at the start of this essay – learning how to spread innovation across the sector faster and better without relying on Whitehall. For many years, councils have complained about the 'tyranny of best practice' – the predilection of government to alight on innovative practice, anoint it with official support and insist it is applied everywhere without regard to variation in local needs or circumstances. Now we have to show we can do better – by developing an approach that both allows councils to develop, with local people, approaches that work locally, and ensures that there is no place untouched by it.

The first step is to ensure that all councils understand that they do not need permission to be ambitious for their communities or to innovate. Their legal powers are wider than they sometimes imagine. In any case, who is going to challenge action that improves services and outcomes or delivers better value for money just because the council responsible has exceeded the scope of its formal powers?

The second step is to encourage all councils to improve their ability to involve and harness the contributions of service users and local residents. Far from being a distraction or burden, user and community involvement – as the best private sector practice reveals – can be a potent source of innovative ideas.

The final step – and this is where the LGA and other central bodies, particularly the Improvement and Development Agency, have most to do – is to put in place a knowledge transfer and networking infrastructure that enables all councils to find out quickly what others are doing, steal ideas from them, share learning on what works and what does not, and apply the lessons. The medical profession has a well-developed infrastructure of respected journals, professional bodies, conferences and other resources for sharing knowledge. As a result, an innovation such as keyhole surgery can spread rapidly throughout the sector without any involvement or intervention from Whitehall. Our ambition must be to match this sector-led support for learning across the local government sector.

Paul Coen is chief executive and Matthew Warburton is head of strategy, Local Government Association.

Notes

1   Communities and Local Government, *Strong and Prosperous Communities: The local government white paper* (Norwich: TSO, 2006).
2   Local Government Association, *The Local Challenge* (London: LGA, 1998).
3   LGA, *Closer to People and Places* (London: LGA, 2006), available at www.lga.gov.uk/Documents/Publication/closertopeople.pdf (accessed 15 Jun 2007).

5. Customer-driven service design

Chris Naylor

In 2002, Hammersmith and Fulham seemed to be in a pretty strong position. We had an 'excellent' rating in the Comprehensive Performance Assessment, we were ahead of the game in terms of partnership working and political governance, we offered reasonable value for money and our key performance indicators were trending up. But behind the scenes things looked less positive. Our customer satisfaction data told us that we had a problem. We weren't doing badly in comparison with other London boroughs, but the figures revealed a growing gap between our self-image as a service provider and the day-to-day experience of our customers. We needed urgently to improve people's experience of the council.

That fact that was brought home powerfully in the 2002 local elections. Confident of their message of success, the then administration returned from the doorstep reeling from the sense of antipathy and in some cases anger that residents expressed about their experience of the council. We weren't answering the phones and, when we did, the caller would often be passed from pillar to post. Our website was inadequate. Why on earth didn't different parts of the council speak to each other and share information?

So in 2003 the council established the Customer First initiative. We entered into a strategic partnership with local firm Agilisys to help us change the way we did business. A few months later we opened a corporate call centre that offered extended opening hours and better call answering times. Grassroots 'Customer First Circles' provided a forum for frontline staff to share their experiences and propose micro-level changes in their workplace to improve the customer experience. There was a buzz about the place. We had opened up the space for innovation within the council and it seemed to be paying off in improved processes.

Two years into the programme, however, our direction of travel was less certain. While our projects and initiatives had delivered benefits, it was clear that there was much further to go. But what exactly should we do next?

While our call centre had improved access to services there was still more to be done in terms of resolving our customers' enquiries at the first point of contact. For example, residents moving in and out of the borough had to contact us numerous times to update or establish their account with the council – be that electoral registration, council tax or applying for a parking permit. Given that 30 per cent of our population move into, within or out of the borough every year surely providing a 'one call and it's done' solution should now become a priority for improvement? Or should our focus turn to the numerous face-to-face reception points dotted around the borough and follow the lead of others and invest in the creation of one or more 'one stop shops'?

All these options had considerable organisational and cost implications. We followed closely the experience of our neighbouring councils who were entering into eye-wateringly long-term out-sourcing deals with the private sector. Was this the right approach for our council and for our customers?

It was clear that we faced some important strategic choices, but we lacked a robust evidence base to help us make them. Conjuring up a wish list of things we could do to improve customer services was one thing. Identifying the optimal mix was quite another. We quickly recognised that we needed a better understanding of who our customers were and how they wanted to interact with our services. We needed to get to know them better if we were going to model the likely impact that different investment options would have on satisfaction. Further innovations would not come solely from within the council, but from a deeper engagement with the people we served – the new strategy would explicitly aim to become 'customer-led'.

By developing a predictive model we would be able to test not only the financial benefits of a particular investment decision, but the impact on customer satisfaction too. In building such a model we understood that we would have to go beyond the standard demographic metrics at our disposal. We would need a different kind of evidence – a sociological set of customer types that would help us understand what was driving satisfaction and dissatisfaction with the council for different groups. Who are our customers? What kind of lives do they lead? What influences their expectation of the council? What really drives their dissatisfaction and ongoing frustration? We needed to understand the answers more deeply, using a wider range of tools.

Our analysis would also need to be grounded in the tangible detail of how council services are currently configured and then presented to our customers. In particular we needed to be clear about how much scope we had to modify or change the way we delivered services. For example, it would be pointless to propose online registration of births and deaths if we were legally prevented from doing that. For reasons like these, we embarked on a customer insight project with the following outcomes in mind:

○   developing a much clearer understanding of who our customers are, based on a segmentation of those residents with similar behaviours, characteristics, needs and aspirations

○   building a model of how our residents access services to identify which services mattered most to which segments, from which locations and over which channels – was it most appropriate to use the phone, the internet, the post? Specifically we wanted to test and understand the nature of customer contact and the nature of the business processes involved – for instance, which channels are most appropriate for different services and different episodes of contact

O applying the model to understand where the council should target its investment to ensure that we delivered both customer satisfaction and efficient services.

Discerning a customer-led strategy

There were three phases to the project. First, we used existing data to build a model of our customers and the way they accessed services. This allowed us to develop some hypotheses about the way people wanted to interact with us, helping us to understand which communication channels different groups preferred, and which clusters of services each group uses most. This gave us an initial sense of how we could group our services into new business units, and which communication channels each business unit should focus on using.

Second, we tested the hypotheses in a survey of 1200 residents of the borough who had used one or more of the council's services in the past year. This allowed us to refine the hypotheses and develop more insights into locations and service groups. Based on this survey, we were able to understand how our citizens would want to access our services in an ideal world.

The final phase was to compare the 'ideal world' model with the way we currently did business, testing its feasibility, understanding what needed to change and getting a better sense of how much we would need to invest to do it, as well as the likely benefits.

At the heart of our strategy was a systematic approach to drawing out three key relationships, namely that between customer and services, customer and communication channel, and between services and communication channel. In other words, we wanted to understand the following:

O Who are our customers and what services do they consume most often?

O   Which communication channels do our customers want
     to use?
O   Which communication channels are feasible or desirable
     for each service?

Our analysis revealed 12 key customer segments within the borough.
For the purposes of developing our customer services strategy, these
were subsequently marshalled into three broader groups.

The biggest group was the 51 per cent of the borough's population
that can broadly be described as 'well off'. They are almost all
professionals, differentiated by whether they have families and
whether they have settled in the borough for the long term. These
customers tend to have busy working lives and consequently have an
inherent preference for internet and phone channels of communication. Coincidentally, they are also the main customers of the
council's more transactional services – parking permit applications,
council tax inquiries, electoral registration and the like. These services
lend themselves to electronic delivery, so the implication for our
strategy was that we should focus investment on improving our web
and phone capability.

The second significant group was the 33 per cent of residents who
could be described as 'deprived' – a combination of students, young
singles, deprived families and older people in sheltered housing.
These groups tend to place multiple demands on social-care-type
services, including adult and children's care, housing, benefits and
aspects of education. This group prefers face-to-face contact, which
reflects the fact that their services require personal interaction, but
can also be due to their lack of access to technology. They are,
however, very willing to use the phone.

Unlike their better-off counterparts, they often use services in
sequence – someone with a disability will often need to interact with
several different parts of the council to resolve an issue. The
implication for our strategy was that we should focus on improving
the quality and coherence of face-to-face and phone contact.

The remaining group – 16 per cent, moderate means to moderately deprived – tended to exhibit behaviours and consumption patterns of both of the above two groups depending on their personal circumstances. Although a simplification of the recommendations of the strategy, we concluded that it would be reasonable to predict that if the satisfaction of the other two groups improved, then it would for this group too.

There were four other important insights:

- ○ All customers wanted to have a single number or point of contact where they can report street scene or environmental issues, graffiti etc. Their expectation is to 'report once and consider it done'.
- ○ Civic-type services – such as registration of births and deaths and democratic engagement-type matters – do not fall within the consumption patterns described above. They share coherence in so far as they reflect the civic nature of the council. From a face-to-face perspective they have a natural home in the 'town hall'.
- ○ Environment services (non street scene) such as planning and development control similarly are not consumed in the patterns identified above. The business process is also quite different, often requiring direct engagement with a professional. There is strong demand to improve web capability for the customers of these services. There is, however, no compelling argument to co-locate these services with other access points. Indeed, the nature of the service is such it would be preferable to maintain a separate face-to-face presence designed specifically for the professional nature of the service enquiries.
- ○ Housing benefit, although most dominantly consumed by the more deprived groups, is much closer in character to the services consumed by the better-off segments. Moreover, we found that customer expectations mirror those of the better off. In applying the data to the future configuration of council services we therefore concluded

that housing benefit (with due consideration to outreach working for the less well off) should be aligned with the provision of other transactional services such as council tax and parking permits, rather than with social-care-type services.

Concluding a customer-led operating model

The final stage of our analysis was to develop a new operating model designed specifically to address the concerns identified by the customer insight data. We needed to re-focus the council's management framework so that the differentiated priorities of our customers could be 'hard wired' into the day-to-day business of the council and its ongoing managerial accountabilities. In other words, we wanted to reflect the affinity of customers to channels, channels to services and services to customers in the way the council operated. In this context we concluded in favour of developing three new business units:

○ Residents Direct
○ Smarter Borough
○ Community Support Centre.

Residents Direct

This is primarily an online and phone-based service supported by a single small-sized reception that was designed to deliver the majority of the council's transactional-type services, in particular council tax, housing benefits, parking permits, applications for other permits and licences, room and appointment bookings, and information and enquiries (such as electoral registration, library opening times, etc).

The operating model for Residents Direct recognises the tension between the generic imperatives of improved customer service and the need to preserve service integrity. This tension is overcome through a matrix operational structure and by ensuring that there is no artificial split between the front office and back office teams. Indeed, the operation of Residents Direct is predicated on the co-location and consolidation of front and back office teams supported by re-engineered business processes and a better deployment of generic and service specialist staff. In effect, there is no front office/back office split.

The management priorities and business objectives of Residents Direct are specifically focused on resolving the frustrations of those better-off segments in the borough who are dissatisfied with the prevalence of face-to-face service provision. The performance management framework for the business unit reflects the imperatives to resolve customer enquiries quickly and correctly. Staff appraisal and development is concentrated on maximising productivity (time-keeping, monitoring the speed and accuracy of enquiry resolution, etc). Investment in IT is aimed at improving 'self-serve' capability on the council's website. The Residents Direct management team is tasked with achieving ambitious medium-term channel transfer targets.

The business case for implementing Residents Direct is predicated on the cashable savings that can be achieved from the consolidation of front and back office operations and on the medium-term achievement of modest transfers of customer transactions to cheaper access channels (specifically the web).

Smarter Borough

This is a web and phone-based service (no face-to-face provision), giving our customers the opportunity to report environment, enviro-crime and anti-social behaviour-type issues. This would include reporting fly tips, graffiti, noise complaints, etc.

In contrast to Residents Direct, the operating design is predicated on a hard front to back office split. Although reported via a single phone number or a single web reporting tool, the resolution of Smarter Borough service requests has to be passed on to an in-house council team (eg enforcement officers) or an externalised service provider (eg street cleansing contractor). It is this feature that distinguishes Smarter Borough from the Residents Direct business unit. In this context the management discipline within the Smarter Borough service is focused on capturing accurately the initial service request and on managing the client–service provider interface. Performance monitoring is focused on improving the speed and accuracy of issue resolution and on the timely feedback of outcomes to customers. Management attention on a day-to-day basis is focused on improving the interplay between separate teams and ensuring that operational practices don't obscure the overall aim of 'putting the customer first'.

The business case for implementing the Smarter Borough business unit is predicated on largely non-cashable savings that can be achieved from better managing the council's client-side relationship with its service providers.

Community Support Centre

This is primarily a face-to-face and limited phone-based service offering customer coherence across adult and children social services and housing-related services. Customers of the Community Support Centre will be able to access, under one roof, the services most often consumed by these customers in a single episode. Over time we will aim to provide services from partner agencies, in particular the local primary care trust, within the Community Support Centre.

The business model is predicated on a consolidation of assessment processes and a simplification of eligibility criteria and proofs of circumstance. As with Residents Direct the tension between professional specialists and better generic working is managed through a matrix management structure supported by a single accountability framework for the overall outcomes of the unit.

The business case for implementing the Community Support Centre is predicated on the cashable savings that can be achieved from the consolidation of front and back office operations and from a significant reduction in the overall accommodation footprint of the in-scope services. There are no channel transfer assumptions included in the business case.

The end of the beginning for using customer insight data

The sceptical observer may consider that the conclusion of our customer services strategy – namely the development of three new customer-led business units – is hardly world changing. In fact, isn't it obvious? There is undoubtedly an intuitive simplicity to our proposals and yet Hammersmith and Fulham is unique among councils in implementing this structure and approach.

Not all of our findings fit with the prevailing wisdom. For instance, the consolidation of front and back office arrangements to form Residents Direct explicitly contradicts the current trend towards splitting front and back office arrangements and achieving savings through shared service arrangements. Not only will Residents Direct achieve better levels of first-contact enquiry resolution in comparison with a 'bog standard call centre', it will also deliver significant financial savings for the council. In its first three years of operation, the business unit will achieve a 20 per cent cashable saving on net costs.

At the heart of our approach has been a simple but rigorous commitment to use customer data to inform both the strategic questions we pose and the method through which we answer them. Had our starting point been an appraisal of the potential of IT or an importation of off-the-shelf customer service paradigms from the private sector then we would have surely concluded a different and arguably less optimal proposition. Having finalised our customer service strategy it is also clear that we have only just scratched the surface of the potential customer metrics can play in improving service design and service outcomes.

Obvious next steps include using our customer segmentation and insight data to improve communication and consultation activity. As our confidence grows we will experiment with differentiated communications material to different postcodes in the borough. Customer data will drive our approach to the personalisation of services and help us understand how best to offer service choice to our customers. A more profound impact could be on wider community governance. As the borough's decision-makers better understand the impact of policy on different customer groups our governance arrangements will need to evolve so that legitimate political challenge can be informed by the totality of customer data available to council leadership.

Chris Naylor is director of resident services, London Borough of Hammersmith and Fulham.

6. Urban innovation and the power of mass imagination

Melissa Mean

Over the last decade our urban faith has been revived by the resurgence and verve of places like London, Manchester, Newcastle Gateshead and Glasgow. Cranes across the skyline, statement architecture, style hotels and Michelin star restaurants are the visible iconography of this new faith, but it is grounded in the now mainstream recognition that cities, rather than firms or the nation-state, are the prime engines of economic innovation and growth.[1] In the creative economy, place matters.

However, there are signs that the space for social, cultural, technological and economic innovation in our cities remains unduly constrained, that following the tightly instrumental reappraisal of the value of cities, something has been lost. As Richard Sennett has written:

> *Something has gone wrong, radically wrong, in our conception of what a city itself should be. We need to imagine just what a clean, safe, efficient, dynamic, stimulating, just city would look like concretely – we need those images to confront critically our masters with what they should be doing – and just this critical imagination of the city is weak.*[2]

In a recent policy briefing, NESTA hinted at the problem. Eight out of nine regional innovation strategies in England pinpoint biotechnology as a priority area. Five out of nine include the creative industries. This reduction of urban innovation to a repetitive formula is part of a wider problem where an institutional view of where innovation takes place and how in cities still dominates. To move on from the 'science park + cultural quarter' formula, we need a better understanding of the relationship between cities and innovation.

Ultimately, we need to find new space and resources to explore and experiment with alternative, more broadly based patterns of innovation. The key will be moving beyond the official future of strategy documents and organograms, and finding new ways to harness the mass imagination and energy of the people who live in cities. This approach creates new opportunities for innovations that can connect economic, social change and citizen aspirations in positive, locally distinctive ways. Without this, there is a danger that the limit of what the current formula can achieve will quickly be reached, and the much trumpeted resurgence of our cities will prove cyclical and short lived rather than structural and sustainable.

The creative age

The resurgence of cities needs to be explained in the context of the rise of the creative age – a long wave of change affecting every sector of the economy. The contrast with the industrial age could not be sharper, as Fredrick Taylor, the American industrial engineer, made brutally clear a hundred years ago:

> *Individual insight is an impediment in the Industrial Age. A good worker is merely a man more or less of the type of an ox, heavy both mentally and physically. Man can become no more than a veritable machine.*[3]

We have moved from an age of mass reproduction where you could have any colour as long as it was black, to an age of mass personalisation and mass customisation. This new pattern of production and growth depends increasingly on an open-ended process of cooperation and collaboration between many different players with tight feedback loops between firms, organisations, suppliers, customers, marketers and the broader environment. Cities matter in the creative age because, at their best, they provide a platform that is well suited to supporting and nourishing this new growth pattern. This capability is predicated on two key qualities: proximity and diversity.

Proximity means cities are able to provide key nodes for the circulation and exchange of people and ideas. Wireless communication, the internet and faster and cheaper air travel have not lessened the importance of proximity and face-to-face contacts, but even seem to encourage it, increasing the magnetic power and stickiness of some places to attract and retain people. But the nature of this proximity is very different from that of the industrial age, where what mattered was proximity to a port and a large fairly homogenous labour market. In the creative economy what counts is proximity to a mix of markets, skills, clients, media, users and customers.

Diversity is vital because it is through combining and colliding new and old that innovation and adaptation occur. The more open a city is to new people, new ideas and new ways of living, the healthier its creative metabolism will be. Richard Florida and his three Ts of Talent, Technology and Tolerance has popularised the importance of openness and tolerance to economic development.[4] Importantly, his research suggests that we should flip the usual assumption of cause and effect: dynamic economies do not beget social cohesion; rather certain kinds of social cohesion can beget dynamic economies.

Mind the gap

The emerging pattern of innovation in cities is then an open and distributed one – an ecology rather than a pipeline.[5] Instead of an elite activity occurring only in special places, it needs to involve many players and to take root in diverse clusters of places and spaces. This is potentially an incredibly democratic and empowering story. However, it is important to take a step back and ask a question: what is all this urban activity and innovation for? For not even the most resurgent of the UK's cities have yet reached a happy ending. Even a cursory survey reveals that despite a rise in prosperity and living standards many are facing a common set of problems including:

○ growing economic, social and spatial inequality
○ deepening divisions and fragmentation within the labour market
○ fragmentation and new class distinctions based on values and life-skills
○ breakdown of trust among people and between people and institutions.

With the emergence, and in some cases reinforcement, of these kinds of complex problems, a gap is emerging between the kinds of cities people want and the places they are currently getting. For example, one recent study of 4.4 million adults in Sweden found that the incidence rates of psychosis and depression rose in proportion with increasing levels of urbanisation.[6]

What has been missing so far in the story about innovation in cities are the human and neighbourhood dimensions. Turning the focus to these issues quickly reveals the sharp mismatch between the language of economic innovation – with its constant references to openness and distribution – and the essentially closed and institutionally dominated nature of much policy-making and governance in our cities.

The official future

This situation is symbolised by the emergence and dominance of the 'official future' in many cities. Told by a spidery organogram of institutions in a web of strategy documents, development plans, mission statements and conference speeches, and woven through every subject area from health to tourism, the official future is a set of implicit assumptions which set and constrain a city's parameters for public participation, strategy and decision-making. While not unified or uniform, many cities' official futures are imbued with a common tone, language and content, and all point in the same direction. The common core themes comprise:

O   step change and transformation
O   a narrowly defined optimism based on economic growth
O   a desire to be world class
O   the language of opportunity and choice but combined with
O   an emphasis on 'one voice, one vision'.

The problem with official futures is that they swallow people's sense of agency. They present a future that has already been decided and leaves little room for people's everyday creativity and aspirations, or the belief that they can positively shape the world around them. This is bad for democracy – and is reflected in the low voter turnouts in cities. But it is also bad for innovation because official futures alienate the most abundant and potent source of new ideas and practices in a city – its people.

To try and find an alternative to the official future, Demos spent 18 months working with Glasgow. Using storytelling and other tools to create a new mental map of the city, the aim was to bring to the surface some new shared stories about the future of the city that could help to counter the forces of fatalism, disconnection and fragmentation.

What people began to create in Glasgow was a new pattern of participation utilising the city's structural qualities of proximity and diversity and involving people outside, within and between institutions. This experiment in mass imagination has some potentially useful lessons for broadening out the discussion and practice of urban innovation in cities to include not just the economic dimensions, but also social and democratic innovation.

A source book for mass imagination

If you want to uncover new stories about the future of a city, then you need to find new ways of inspiring and asking for those stories. Fostering the public imagination requires working at different scales across the city, with established communities and emerging ones, in the spaces between large institutions, community groups and individuals. It requires working firmly in the public arena but also maintaining a level of personal intimacy.

The following design principles are grounded in the methodology of the mass imagination project Demos led in Glasgow. They are offered as a source book for other neighbourhoods, towns and cities that are interested in the creation of an independent, creative public space for people to imagine the future together and new ideas for living together.

1. Network logic

The critical element in a city-wide process of mass imagination is people. Instead of expecting people to come to you, you need to work with and through trusted intermediaries and existing relationships to invite people and communities to take part.

In Glasgow, the core project team was supported by 20 public, private and voluntary sector organisations and their extensive networks in the city. In addition we worked with a wider and looser network of collaborators including community and youth groups, hair salons, cafés and artists. The result was a project that was able to connect with the formal Glasgow of council officers and chief executives, but could also reach out to people in galleries and libraries, people in tower blocks and outlying estates, people on public transport, people in cafés and bars, as well as people in the Gambia, Amsterdam, Helsinki, Gothenburg and Stockholm.

2. Imagination not consultation

The last decade has seen a greater emphasis on community involvement in decision-making in an effort to make a break from some of the socially divisive urban policies of the 1980s and 1990s. However, consultation has often proved frustrating in practice with – at best – a great deal of ambiguity about how much real power or freedom communities have to influence decisions. Instead of starting with a pre-set agenda, mass imagination is about starting with the issues that people come across in their everyday lives.

Demos used two main tools to help open the conversation up: narrative and culture. Narrative because it is the natural way that people communicate and understand the world around them. Culture because increasingly culture is proving a far more effective way to inspire collective experiences than our current political or policy language. Some 38 events were run in total, none of which had a pre-set agenda other than to explore Glasgow's future. Tools such as storytelling, role-playing, drawing and animation were used to facilitate the discussion.

3. Different strokes for different folk

If a process of mass imagination is to be truly public it needs to have many different ways for people to participate. One of the most accessible elements in Glasgow 2020 was a campaign inviting people to make a wish for the kind of city they wanted in 2020.

Freepost postcards were distributed in public buildings around the city – people could write their wishes on the postcards and send them back. A giant wishbook toured schools, offices and public buildings collecting people's wishes. People could submit their wish on the project website, where they could be viewed and rated by other visitors. Finally, all the six-year-olds living in Glasgow (who will turn 21 in 2020) were written to and invited to make a wish – over 1000 of them did so.

4. Using disruptive spaces and everyday spaces

Mass imagination does not happen just in committee rooms and community halls – we need to take the conversation beyond these spaces. The Glasgow project did this in two ways. First, it took discussions about the future of the city into the everyday public spaces of the city – into hair salons, cafés, libraries and museums, in order to tap into the bottom-up intelligence of the city. This also signalled that the shared future of Glasgow was not a closed game to be played in smoke-filled rooms by experts and grandees, but instead a tangibly public enterprise.

Second, the project set up a series of 'disruptive spaces' to explore the future of the city. These experimental events helped to open up different perspectives and conversations as the unusual setting encouraged people to be more open. The disruptive events included turning a boat into a free office for a day; taking over trains between Glasgow and Edinburgh for two days and three cargo cabins filled with art being installed in different neighbourhoods across Glasgow; and 'The Big Dream', an interactive festival at the Kelvingrove Art Gallery and Museum.

The aim with all the events was to create a 'trading zone' where different people could come together as equals and exchange different experiences, beliefs and hopes about the future of Glasgow. Harvard Professor Peter Galison coined the term to describe places that are 'partly symbolic and partly spatial – at which the local coordination between beliefs and actions takes place'.[7]

5. An open tool box

Mass imagination is not something to be guarded defensively. It is a public good: the more open it is and the more it is given away, the stronger it becomes. Therefore the process of imagining the future cannot be totally owned by the organisation starting it. It needs to be something that different people and organisations can pick up and run with.

Glasgow 2020 openly publicised the fact that it was ready to support any individuals or organisations who were interested in doing their own Glasgow 2020 event. A range of events happened like this including a series of discussions in a women's library, a visioning process by the Port of Glasgow community, and a neighbourhood church's summer school, which created a giant 3D model of the city in 2020.

6. The freedom of information

Public imagination is not a process that can or should have one narrator. The role of Demos was that of facilitators and animators, helping people themselves to understand, articulate and exchange their own views and hopes for the future of Glasgow. It is also important that the process is transparent and that stories and ideas are able to circulate, helping prompt further reflection and development of new ideas.

The project encouraged three different spheres of conversation. First, the public sphere comprised of the make-a-wish campaign, the story-writing competitions, the media partnership and coverage with the main city newspaper, the *Evening Times*, and a dedicated website. Second was the community sphere with events with specific groups. Third was the official sphere with institutions and public organisations.

The circulation of ideas between the three spheres was encouraged. So, for example, wishes and elements of stories submitted were used as starting points for discussions in workshops. These workshops produced stories, which in turn were given to authors who developed particular characters and storylines into complete narratives. These stories were then distilled into seven emerging storylines for the future, which were publicly tested and refined at the public event at Kelvingrove Art Gallery and Museum to which over 700 people came.

The combination of these six principles adds up to a project that is partly a campaign (it sought to enlist people in futures thinking), partly a public culture project (it engaged people's imagination) and partly a piece of policy research (it generated learning for the development of urban policy and practice).

From storylines to action

The stories Glasgow's people created, the wishes they cast and their myriad discussions did not create a single unifying vision for the city. Instead a more complex and diverse set of storylines emerged from which seven possible scenarios can be distilled for what Glasgow could be like in 2020. The headline scenarios are:

○ *The Two-Speed City* – Glasgow becomes a place divided between rich and poor.
○ *The Soft City* – The city's hard, masculine attitudes are

replaced by a more feminine feel, with conversation, verve and cooperation becoming key themes.

O   *The Hard City* – The city authorities lose patience with their people's unruliness and become ever more authoritarian.

O   *The Dear Green City* – Industrial Glasgow has been replaced with a fierce pride in greenness and sustainability, becoming self-sufficient in energy terms.

O   *The Slow City* – The city rejects harsh consumerism and spends more of its time caring for children, neighbours and the elderly.

O   *The Lonely City* – Glasgow's sense of community is on the wane as people increasingly socialise through their computers.

O   *The Kaleidoscope City* – Glasgow has become a kaleidoscope of diversity, thriving off its ability to absorb new waves of immigration from across the globe.

These emergent storylines blend radical change and conservative nostalgia; a heady brew of hopes and fears for what the future might hold. Together they represent a significant opening up of the urban imagination about the kinds of lives – individual and collective – people hope are possible in our cities. At the same time, they expose a sharp ingenuity gap between people's hoped-for futures and the current set of tools and resources available to get them there.

Progressing any of the emergent storylines – or averting any of them – requires more than just opening up space for non-institutional voices and storylines. It also requires finding new ways to mobilise communities of interest and action behind those storylines. It demands developing new patterns of participation and new patterns of producing collective goods. If the first step to a better future is imagining one, then the next step is about collaboration, where institutional Glasgow is only one player among many. We need to make the crucial move from mass imagination to mass collaboration, involving local government and the voluntary sector, but not necessarily led by them.

The experience of the Glasgow project indicates that the energy and optimism is out there to begin to do this. One of the most powerful findings of the project was the desire people have for contexts and spaces where they can begin now to experiment with, build and progress some of the better futures they imagined:

> *The big chances for changes don't lie with the council – but with ourselves. We need to do stuff to live together better, and not just look to the political system to change us.*
>
> Male westender

> *People start using their imagination and positive attitude to change things for themselves. Teenagers stop complaining they've got nothing to do and create things for themselves. . . . People start working on it and set [an] example to others.*
>
> Teenager in Govan

This becomes even more interesting when combined with the sharp contrast we found in Glasgow with the new orthodoxy that we are a society of 'lucky pessimists' – essentially that we are optimistic about our own futures, but sceptical about the prospects of improvement for public services and society as a whole. In Glasgow, we found people were almost as optimistic about the future of the city as they were about their own lives – a net optimism rating of +55.5 and +60.2, respectively.

This potentially opens up a new, richer story about innovation, one that connects individual and collective wellbeing through the collective institution of the city, but goes far wider and deeper than the town hall, or indeed science parks and cultural quarters.

Melissa Mean is head of the cities programme at Demos.

Notes

1   See for example, HM Treasury, *Devolving Decision Making: Meeting the regional economic challenge – the importance of cities to regional growth* (London: HM Treasury, 2006).

2   R Sennett, 'The open city', Urban Age discussion paper, see www.urban-age.net/0_downloads/Berlin_Richard_Sennett_2006-The_Open_City.pdf (accessed 16 Jun 2007).

3   FW Taylor, *The Principles of Scientific Management* (New York: Harper Bros, 1911).

4   R Florida, *The Rise of the Creative Class* (New York: Basic Books, 2002).

5   NESTA, *The Innovation Gap: Why policy needs to reflect the reality of innovation in the UK* (London: National Endowment for Science, Technology and the Arts, 2006), available at: www.nesta.org.uk/assets/pdf/innovation_gap_report_NESTA.pdf (accessed 11 Apr 2007).

6   K Sundquist, G Frank and J Sundquist, 'Urbanisation and incidence of psychosis and depression: follow-up study of 4.4 million women and men in Sweden', *British Journal of Psychiatry* 184 (2004).

7   P Galison, *Image and Logic* (Chicago: Chicago University Press, 1997).

7. Innovation in public–private partnerships

Ian Keys and Roger O'Sullivan

For all the rhetoric, innovation in public–private partnerships (PPPs) is relatively rare. There are two principal reasons for this. First, public sector contracting is still heavily influenced by its roots in asset procurement – for most of the last century, local and central government focused heavily on buying new public infrastructure, schools, hospitals and military equipment. Second, many public organisations still have negative attitudes towards PPPs after the trauma of enforced competitive tendering in the 1990s. The Major government was much more interested in cost reductions than innovative service improvement, while councils resented being forced to outsource their services and consequently became controlling and antagonistic towards private-sector partners. In these circumstances, innovation became immensely difficult.

Some real strides have been made since the suspension of competitive tendering in 1997 – the government has increasingly tried to prioritise quality as well as cost, and the debate about PPPs has matured significantly. Today, private companies like our own are not seen as a threat or a way of doing services on the cheap, but increasingly as a genuine partner to local and central government in improving service delivery. Independent evidence has shown that the more competitive a council is in its approach to service provision, the more likely it is that it will improve overall.

For all that positive change, the public sector has still not fully made the transition from procuring assets to managing services. Business is still asked to respond to tenders that specify in quite some detail what we have to deliver. We are asked to respond to the client's ideas about service improvement, with little opportunity to bring established industry best practice to bear. Once we have won a tender we have precious little opportunity to vary the service to meet the needs of the people we serve. The result is incremental improvement in quality and cost, rather than the 'transformation' that many public sector clients claim to want.

Many private providers may like it this way – the current contractual model gives them stability and allows them to implement relatively straightforward and standardised business models that yield quick results when applied to poor public-sector performers. That approach may have been the right one in the past. The early 2000s were a period in which many councils and other parts of the public sector needed urgently to improve their services.

But things are changing – local government performance has risen very significantly in the past decade, to the extent that many councils have already implemented basic good practice. What they need now are innovative new approaches that can push them further. In particular, they need to find new ways to reconnect with their customers, whose satisfaction has continued to fall despite improved performance by local government. As one evaluation of the local government modernisation agenda put it:

Much of the progress made so far has been achieved by encouraging poor performing authorities to conform to a model of 'modern local government' which involves adopting existing good practice – at corporate and service levels . . . [but now] bolder experimentation and innovation and more fundamental changes in cross-boundary working are needed to encourage more rapid improvement.[1]

In many service areas we are reaching the limits of centrally driven improvement and we need to open up the space to try new solutions on the ground. Local government already has a well-established mixed economy of service provision, so it is becoming urgent that we address not just how public sector organisations can become aware of industry best practice, but how we create the space for innovation to happen through PPPs.

What is required is nothing less than a fundamental shift in contracting models. We need to reject the 'not invented here' mentality, encouraging councils to integrate industry best practice in their work. We need to break down rigid, legalistic approaches to contracting and adopt much more flexible and adaptive models that allow the private sector to work with service users to innovate and drive citizen-focused improvements. And we need to see the inclusion of a profound dialogue stage in procurement processes, with public and private honestly discussing their capabilities and needs well before a tender is even issued. This would mean that when the tender is issued, it reflects an up-to-date knowledge of what the industry is capable of and what it has achieved elsewhere.

Of course, this is not a challenge just for the public sector. Business and the voluntary sector also need to become more willing to engage in speculative dialogue and to share their own best practice. The contracting industry needs to become more open and discursive and it also needs to recognise the need to work harder and take risks to deliver ever-more innovative service offerings. Dialogue, innovation and collaboration should become the watchwords of this new era of contracting.

A new approach to creating innovative PPPs will create risks for both contractor and client that should not be underplayed, but the potential rewards are very worthwhile. Tight contracts, which both sides hide behind when the going gets tough, will become a thing of the past and a more flexible, responsive and public-value-based model will emerge.

Finding examples of this new approach operating in practice is not easy – the climate for innovation in PPPs is only now beginning to improve. One place we might look for evidence to support a new model of contracting is in the experience of tenant management organisations (TMOs), which allow social housing tenants to take control of their own estates.

The tenant management organisation experience

TMOs provide us with a good place to start learning about innovation in partnership. Because they are owned and managed by residents, they create the opportunity for direct dialogue with service users and the legitimacy to change and adapt the services provided over time. They are a powerful example partly because they show how PPP models can support greater democracy as well as the delivery of better, more responsive, public services.

Since 1994, council tenants have had a legal 'right to manage' their estates and more than 200 groups have set up TMOs to do so, with funding support from the government. The oldest TMO is in Kensington and Chelsea in London. Set up in 1996 with the housing stock transferring from the council, it manages around 10,000 homes and has just been awarded 'three stars with excellent prospects for improvement'. This is the highest possible rating that can be awarded by the Audit Commission and only a handful of housing organisations nationally of any kind have achieved such an accolade.[2]

The Housing Corporation[3] suggests that people should set up TMOs to:

O make sure things are done that are important for the community and are not being done by others
O bring local people together and help create a sense of identity which may have been absent before; it can focus people's minds as well as their efforts on tackling issues collectively
O encourage people to develop a sense of pride, community spirit and togetherness that may have been absent for many years
O offer new job opportunities for the non-joiners in local

communities to get involved and feel included, rather than excluded

O make sure local services really do meet community needs, by relying less on outside bodies

O empower individuals, enabling them to use skills they never knew they had, or develop new ones

O produce a great feeling of a satisfaction in people who are doing things for themselves and achieving things, perhaps for the first time

O create local jobs.

The success of TMOs as a way of engaging the public and improving housing was recognised in the recent local government white paper,[4] which promises to make them easier to set up. Business has played a role in this success, taking on TMO services, which range from housing management and repairs to childcare provision and activities for young people.

The Clapton Park TMO

Pinnacle – the company we work for – manages in whole or in part over 390,000 social homes nationwide. We currently work for 14 TMOs, 7 per cent of the total, and each relationship is underpinned by a partnering contract. Explicitly included within each contract is a requirement that we will seek continually to improve the lives of the local community and save costs. These are profound drivers for service innovation.

We took over housing management in Clapton Park – part of the London Borough of Hackney – in January 2006. The service was outsourced after a critical best-value review, so we decided to assess quickly the extent of the financial and managerial difficulties that were affecting the TMO. Both required serious and urgent attention and a radically different approach.

The key thing that allowed us to innovate in Clapton Park was the relationship we established with the TMO board, which is made up of residents, councillors and a Pinnacle member of staff. We operate under a very traditional PPP contract and have to show that we are meeting its key performance indicators (KPIs), but in practice neither Pinnacle nor residents look at the document very much.

Instead, we put together an annual plan around Christmas in partnership with the board that sets out what we have achieved in the past year and the improvements we intend to deliver in the next. We agree the plan and then help residents secure the necessary money from the council. Once the budget is agreed, Pinnacle gets exceptional flexibility about how to spend the money to deliver the services. This annual plan has become the key document we use to manage the service, with the board itself agreeing the KPIs every year. This allows us to develop our offering in partnership with residents.

When we began the contract, we knew that building a successful relationship depended on our ability to deliver the basics to a very high standard – we needed residents to be able to take good performance for granted. It is a measure of our success that the key topics of conversation at board meetings today are engaging residents in decision-making and regenerating the area, rather than service standards. But the nature of the TMO meant that we could not unilaterally impose radical new approaches from the start. Resident reaction to the service re-engineering we planned with the TMO's board was key: get it right and they would critique what we were doing from a positive standpoint. Get it wrong and obstacles and confusion would get in our way. A radical approach may be logically what is required, but selling the need for it and ensuring public buy-in were, perhaps, even more essential.

Through engagement with residents' groups we checked out our impressions of the weaknesses in the current services and found that the underlying problem was that many of the staff had become leaderless, stale and removed from the TMO's objectives. Increasing amounts of TMO time were being spent on managing de-motivated, unskilled staff rather than on setting service priorities. The staff had become a rudderless ship drifting away from its origins with little directional steer.

With the residents on our side, or at least prepared to give us the benefit of the doubt, Pinnacle set to work. In our experience, both staff and residents want to see quick and successful changes that foster their sense of confidence in the more profound changes that will follow. In Clapton Park, this meant that we committed ourselves to delivering our promises, acting quickly and being honest and open about what we could and could not do, and sharing the reasons why.

The area has some 1150 social homes and when we took over the TMO services, those houses were being maintained expensively, relying on last-minute fixes and with no long-term strategy for improvement. The services that were being provided to the TMO were reactive, uncoordinated and largely unaccountable. The physical fabric of the estate was in need of improvement, repair and regeneration. Residents had complained bitterly about the vandalism that had occurred over the years.

They were used to venting their anger face-to-face, so we decided that one of the first things we should do to make an impact was to install a brand new neighbourhood office. It would become easily accessible and welcoming to visitors, especially those who needed encouragement and support to access services. There would be new opening times that suited visitors – including weekends – and it would have a much more open feel, involving the removal of the office counter and the creation of an open-plan office with staff in public view.

Our next step was to focus our services around the customer. This involved bringing the services most used or talked about by residents into the refurbished office, including cleaning, repairs, rent collection, parking and other housing management activities. A single visit to the office would mean that the resident could deal with whatever problem or query they had there and then. We also put in place a new customer charter setting out Pinnacle standards and promises with a service guarantee and a native-speaking housing officer to engage in depth with the area's Turkish speakers.

The Pinnacle re-engineering has reduced service costs substantially with no service loss. This involved a basic re-think of the way things were done, aimed at putting in place a problem-solving and flexible 'can do' culture. We did this by examining all staff roles and how they were linked to TMO priorities: essentially, we made a fresh start with a blank sheet of paper.

Staff are the key resource in the delivery of any customer-facing activity and from the start we put in place a strategy to take them along with us. This involved building their confidence through putting in place a new management team, talking up the benefits of cultural change, removing the fear inherent in the change to a 'can do' attitude and always being sensitive to the need for a value for money approach.

Many staff were just in need of a change to re-awaken their enthusiasm and through direct dialogue and listening to the views of the TMO committee, over 70 per cent of the existing staff took opportunities elsewhere in Pinnacle, allowing space for fresh ideas and new ways of working to be put in place in the TMO through training and re-skilling. All individual staff now had a visible purpose, transparent objectives and agreed deliverables and each team had defined objectives to deliver. And all of this flowed from the aims and objectives of the TMO board and regular and inclusive evaluation sessions reviewed outputs and outcomes against the resources and skills required.

Performance in all KPIs has improved significantly and resident satisfaction levels are higher, despite the reduction in costs. Revenue from rents has increased and there are fewer empty properties.

Service innovation lessons from the TMO experience

The kind of innovation enabled by TMOs matters because of its potential to create more of what the management theorist Mark Moore has termed 'public value' – essentially the process of identifying, refining and delivering more of the things that people want from their services.[5]

Moore identifies a 'strategic triangle' of three factors that are necessary to deliver this kind of value. The private sector has traditionally specialised in only one of these factors: it often delivers superb operational capacity. Essentially, the private sector is good at getting things done. But Moore argues that two other factors are necessary. Managers need to take on a public value mindset, seeking out the things that the public value most, recognising that these might include fairness, trust and quality of public engagement, and seeking to deliver more of those things. Finally, managers need to get close to their authorising environment – the people and organisations that create the legitimacy for change.

TMOs show that it is possible to match the private sector's delivery expertise with a particular mindset and a close relationship with clients and residents to deliver innovations that increase public value. There are some powerful lessons that all players in the PPP market can take from this experience:

○ Close working relationships between clients, service users and private sector partners need to be built in from the start of a contracting process. The first step is early dialogue with potential bidders to ensure that the tender reflects the very best practice available. The second is to identify a contractor whose values and experience resonate with those of the client and the local community. Finally, the contracting relationship needs to allow for regular dialogue and flexibility that can authorise changes, innovations and improvements to the service.

○ The people who use a service must not be taken for granted – innovations are likely to work most effectively when local residents have a sense of ownership of the changes being proposed. Similarly, client organisations like councils, hospitals and even TMO boards have a wealth of experience that PPPs can harness to help improve services, and they are vital partners in service design, setting goals and legitimising change. By handing over control of the day-to-day tasks of service delivery, clients can often focus more effectively on strategy.

○ Everyone involved in a PPP needs to recognise that public value, efficiency and quality improvements can be delivered only if the service is constantly seeking to reinvent itself. This means that PPPs need to be dynamic and flexible – too much rigidity or too little imagination will stifle real improvements in the long run.

Conclusion

The business world historically has tended to outpace public services in terms of innovation, but this is now changing and concrete examples of service innovation in public sector services are beginning to come through as outdated contracting structures and attitudes are gradually replaced.

Key to this is an early and deep dialogue between the public sector organisation and its prospective private and third-sector partners that aims to create contracts based on citizen-centred services and industry best practice, rather than simply client-originated 'good ideas'. This dialogue phase also needs to involve direct engagement with service users, which will help refine tenders and raise awareness of an impending PPP among local people. This model is now gaining currency among central government departments and forms part of the thinking behind the recent local government white paper.

Moreover, a re-focused procurement process is likely to energise participants, unleashing pent-up frustrations across the private and third sectors in the form of renewed creativity and enthusiasm. This would lead to further innovation arising during the bid construction process – we are likely to see individual companies and charities offering the public sector a wider range of options through what are called 'variant bids' in procurement parlance.

Demands on the public sector and their expectations of public services are both continually changing and becoming increasingly driven by exemplary customer management in the commercial sector. The continued credibility of publicly funded services requires that those services remain appropriate, flexible, responsive and values-based, too. Our citizens as both customers and taxpayers expect nothing less.

Ian Keys is external affairs director and Roger O'Sullivan is managing director, facilities management, Pinnacle.

Notes

1   S Martin and T Bovaird, *Meta-evaluation of the Local Government Modernisation Agenda: Progress report on service improvement in local government* (London: Office of the Deputy Prime Minister, 2006).

2   For further details see www.rbkc.gov.uk/Housing/TMO/default.asp (accessed 17 Jun 2007).

3   Housing Corporation, 'What is community control?', Confederation of Co-operative Housing and the Housing Corporation, March 2003, available at www.communitiestakingcontrol.org/downloads/What_Is_Community_Control.pdf (accessed 17 Jun 2007).

4   Communities and Local Government, *Strong and Prosperous Communities: The local government white paper* (Norwich: TSO, 2006).

5   M Moore, *Creating Public Value* (London: Harvard University Press, 1995).

The strategic centre

8. Twenty-first-century civil servants

The story of MindLab
Mette Abrahamsen

MindLab was established in 2002 as an in-house growth house for innovation at the Ministry of Economic and Business Affairs in Denmark. The aim of MindLab is to raise the capability of innovation among the 2500 civil servants throughout the ministry, while developing new policy and strategies for central government. MindLab's main function is to facilitate the meeting of different cultures in the ministry, through establishing a neutral zone for collaboration and learning. It exists to encourage civil servants to use their creative, as well as their rational, competencies in the development of policy initiatives that meet the needs of citizens and business.

This morning is no different from many other mornings. I enter MindLab, put on the lights. I take a look at the scribbles on the wall which capture the essence of a dialogue that took place here yesterday, among a project team of five civil servants from two different agencies. They were talking about some quite complex issues around the new programme for entrepreneurship, and identifying the different needs that Danish entrepreneurs might have. As the facilitator, I had a hard time trying to get the team to deal with the substance of the issue. Why is this initiative important? What kind of problem is it going to solve? The team was mostly focusing on the political process and the challenge of how to battle with the bad guys at another ministry. Eventually, they managed to develop a list of all the crucial knowledge they didn't have. The team then had some quite tough discussions about how to interpret the latest brief from the minister and how the feasibility study was going to be set up.

Is this innovation? Probably not, at least for the moment. Yesterday was just the warm up, and now the project team is due to arrive again in about an hour. Today we are going to improve the ideas, and start testing the early concepts. But we won't be doing this in the way the team is used to working: it is going to be in front of a real live audience of entrepreneurs – the people who are going to have to live with the new initiative.

I change the scene through setting up four different kinds of user profiles, posters describing different generic types of entrepreneurs who are going to be affected by the new initiative. Each profile describes the needs, worries and of course some basic demographic facts for a particular group. Sometimes we use real citizens, through conducting interviews, or through inviting them to generate ideas together with the team. This seems such a simple and common-sense idea. And yet in most government bureaucracies, it is not a part of the culture to actually listen or ask questions of the people who are going to live with your policies. As a civil servant it is sometimes a little overwhelming facing the 'customer'. It is my job as the facilitator to create a trusting environment where this kind of working is possible.

That is because for meaningful innovation to happen, it is crucial that new ideas are developed on the basis of needs, whether those needs are known or tacit to the users. As the facilitator I have to find a way of bringing the hands-on knowledge of the users into the innovation process in such a way that this kind of knowledge is as highly appreciated as the statistical and analytical data which the civil servants already have, and are usually more comfortable with.

In a short while, I will be asking the team to test their ideas on the different user profiles. They will then spend the rest of the day fleshing out the ideas, turning them into concepts for implementation. Towards the end of the day I will announce another challenge: that they have to present their implementation strategy to the minister, who will be paying MindLab a visit. OK, so usually it is one of my colleagues who plays the minister – but the presentation is for real. We want the team to ask themselves: 'How does the concept sound in a political context?'

The place of MindLab and facilitators like me is to carry teams through a process which gives them the very best platform, not only for implementing new initiatives, but for doing that in the smartest possible way. A way that ensures the intention and spirit of the idea is actually converted into practice that works. That's the reason we involve both the end users and the minister in our process.

Innovation, for me, is about doing it better than you ever thought possible. In my experience the most beneficial way to get to that point is to explore the needs of users at a very early stage of the policy development process. And that is basically what MindLab does. It helps civil servants at the Ministry of Economic and Business Affairs get a grip on their users' needs at an earlier stage than they ever did before.

How did MindLab begin?

When MindLab opened in February 2002, it wasn't breaking news in itself. Many private companies have their own internal units supporting and initiating R&D activities. What made MindLab unique was the fact that it grew out of a demand for facilitation and focus on innovation in a ministry, rather than a commercial firm looking to improve its position in the marketplace.

As with many initiatives in central government, the motivation for investing in MindLab grew out of a cocktail of different needs. How could a ministry which claims to be the guardian of business affairs have any legitimacy with its key stakeholders if it can't manage to run a project organisation or have any kind of systematic innovation process? Even though the ministry had already made several major organisational changes to respond to these challenges – including the introduction of project working, mobility programmes for civil servants and a leadership academy – the feeling was that innovation cannot occur on its own. It seemed to be the right time to raise the organisation's capability, both in terms of creative skills and an innovation methodology. Our ambition was to change the culture throughout the organisation, rather than in just a few dedicated innovation spots.

At a more pragmatic level there was a genuine need for support for civil servants who were trying to navigate and respond to an incredibly complex surrounding environment. They needed hands-on experience in how to develop new and powerful ideas. These ideas not only had to be great in themselves, they also had to be able to survive the process of political negotiation and to become real, practical, working policies.

It is true that there was also a 'nice to have' element behind the decision to create MindLab. The ministry wanted to challenge the commonly held prejudice that the public sector is bureaucratic, grey, boring and ineffective.

Out of all these different needs grew the idea of designing a place, a Lab, which could not only symbolise innovation in itself, but actually foster real, practical innovation. More specifically, we thought about the need to support innovation throughout the ministry by facilitating the early – and from the perspective of the innovation theory, the most vulnerable – phases of projects. MindLab is situated, physically and organisationally, at the Ministry of Economic and Business Affairs, but all the agencies of the ministry have access.

MindLab comprises only a handful of staff. We have an interdisciplinary team of four people, all of whom represent different skills, perspectives and world views from most civil servants. The four profiles are:

○ culture coach – the teamwork expert
○ innovation coach – who has academic skills in innovation
○ planner – the expert in project work
○ policy coach – the 'translator', the one who is most like the other civil servants.

All members of the MindLab team are highly skilled facilitators, and to a different degree we each have analytical competencies in ethnographic research and qualitative analysis. It is the project teams we work with who bring the expertise and knowledge on the particular issue. They will always own the project, and we will be there to provide and inject new perspectives, a facilitated process and a safe challenge.

A neutral zone in a ministry

The 'nice to have' rationale for MindLab turned out to be of much greater importance than anybody ever imagined. Designed by the artists Bosch and Fjord, MindLab became much more than just a funky place. The space itself facilitated innovation and new ideas: it is both a room that seizes a moment, and a toolbox with all the kit you'll ever need for setting up an innovation workshop.

We describe the MindLab space's functionality with the metaphor of the body. At the one end of MindLab there's the 'mind' – a huge egg-shaped sculpture made for brainstorming. You can write on the curved white walls inside the Mind, and it is cocooned from the rest of the world. After the brainstorm we and the team will digest the ideas that have been generated at the 'stomach' – the kitchen you find right in the middle of MindLab. While shaping the ideas, and prioritising them, you should get a good feeling in your stomach. Somebody called this intuition, but I think it's the feeling that we get when rationality meets creativity, when there is some kind of meaning and direction in what we are doing. Finally, the team enters the 'feet', the meeting room of MindLab that is situated at the far end of the room from the mind. Here is the place for planning, doing and action.

This metaphor of the body symbolises the innovation process we use, from idea to reality. What is powerful about the space – apart from being completely different from most offices – is that is makes everybody who enters the room aware of the challenge of innovation. Creativity isn't enough and rationality certainly isn't enough. Innovation needs both.

That said, in practice, we don't do that many brainstorms in the 'mind'. We will usually end up building a workshop zone, or spending time in the kitchen. These are by far the cosiest and most effective places to work. Why is this? I believe it is because when you are letting user needs into the development process earlier, when you are creating a collaborative working environment, then you are also opening up more channels for uncertainty, failure and insecurity about the fact that linear thinking is insufficient, and success rests on the team, not just you. And that way of working is not simply about skills; it is about trust. And MindLab, as a room, feels like a comfortable and trusting place to be. For civil servants, that kind of atmosphere is essential if the skills of working more creatively are to grow.

Reflections on innovation

What we have learnt from the early years of MindLab is that this kind of innovation hub is not just about creating a free-for-all hub of creativity within an otherwise bureaucratic organisation. Instead, we need to combine an innovative approach with the positive dimensions of bureaucracy, such as common sense functionality, as a means of organising and disciplining innovation. As an example, the process of identifying projects to enter the MindLab process is a bureaucratic one based on prioritisation and 'objective' criteria. And yet those criteria include a requirement that every project involves at least two different organisational units. Each project has to be able to express its short- and long-term impacts in terms of the strategic priorities of the ministry. In other words, you need creativity *and* bureaucracy, combined in the right way, to make innovation happen. The problem is that government is often uncertain about how to bring the best elements together at each stage of a project.

The risk of this uncertainty is that innovation is valued only in the process of generating solutions, rather than being seen as something that needs to happen at the point of defining and identifying problems as well. This is exacerbated by the separation of organisational and strategic processes, where the former is held by the civil servants, and the latter by our politicians. Of course, anyone who has ever worked in central government knows that in practice this distinction is often blurred, and kept alive only on a rhetorical level. The challenge therefore is to find ways of allowing innovation into every dimension of the organisation's work, from strategy and problem definition right through to solutions assembly and implementation. MindLab demonstrates that one way to meet this challenge is to create a project process that brings together all stakeholders, and finds a way of speaking in different modes while keeping the ultimate vision vivid.

In the spring of 2006 the first evaluation of MindLab was carried out. By analysing the 300-or-so completed projects (workshops, seminars and research), a web-based survey and interviews, the conclusion was that MindLab had managed to fulfil some of its goals. MindLab has fostered more creativity in the ministry in general. It has been a successful part of a 'bottom-up' process in the ministry for familiarising hundreds of civil servants with their own creative capacity, and encouraging those civil servants to see this creativity as part of doing their job. Increasingly, the ministry's staff is recognising the value of understanding the needs of civil society and their own users as a means of developing better-quality policy.

In other words, it would be possible to say that the success of MindLab so far can be interpreted mainly as discrete experiences among each of the project teams that have worked with us. However, in my view, the kind of individual capacity we helped to build can really reach its full potential only if the overarching organisation has a degree of understanding about the nature of innovation, and a good appetite for organisational change and learning in general. This is the case in the Ministry of Economic and Business Affairs: as MindLab has grown, it has been busy developing systematic procedures and approaches to ensure that it nurtures and grows the innovation skills of its staff.

That said, there is still a need for the ministry to take more of its own medicine. The evaluation also concluded that MindLab has not managed to influence the ways in which the ministry measures a successful project or policy initiative, for example through greater use of user-generated metrics. More needs to be done, in other words, to define innovation as a major, manifest, strategic priority – from the top down as well as the bottom up.

The response to this evaluation is itself a symbol of the ministry's willingness to learn, and the organisational appetite for innovation. MindLab is currently going through its own innovation process, to build up a refreshed unit that will serve the Ministry of Taxation and the Ministry of Labour, as well as the Ministry for Economic and Business Affairs. With this expanded remit will come an even stronger focus on our users. We will be there to focus on 'user-driven innovation to meet public needs'. This approach will need us to bring more analysis and research work in-house, so we will be growing our core team. All of this will be done by the end of 2007.

Like any organisation, whatever its sector, public sector bodies have to grapple with the clash between bottom-up and top-down processes. But what the public sector has that is unique is the need to deal with the separation between the political process and the bureaucratic policy process. This division of strategy and innovation is a very real challenge. What MindLab has shown is that if we trust our civil servants, if we show our confidence in them, then they can and will improve their own capacity to innovate on the basis of user needs. 'Trust' is the keyword in all of this. Change is not driven by systems, but rather by people who find themselves trusted. Systems only help people to innovate. The rest is just hard work.

Mette Abrahamsen was the lead consultant at MindLab. She is now working at Arkitema. Christian Basson is the new director of innovation at MindLab. For more information please visit the website www.mindlab.dk/inenglish/

9. Reforming through technology

Rob Watt

Innovation is the key to the competitiveness of businesses and of nations. A strong and well-developed innovation system and culture underpins economic growth and social wellbeing, particularly when new ideas and technologies are applied to public service delivery. In July 2006, the National Audit Office found that there are five fundamental reasons why the public sector seeks to create change and innovate.[1] These are:

- ○ to meet political decisions and policy change
- ○ to improve service quality to meet targets
- ○ to make services more responsive to the citizen
- ○ to meet public expectations of service standards
- ○ to meet public service agreements and improving service effectiveness.

The report draws a distinction between two different approaches to innovation in government. Some policy changes encourage innovation which improves the effectiveness of the service outcome. Others are initiated within the organisational structure of departments and are aimed primarily at improving productivity and efficiency.

Technology has an important role to play in both of these approaches – by importing best practice from the commercial sector, government institutions can realise significant benefits. But we believe there is a third and under-exploited form of innovation: the public sector should also be involved in developing its own disruptive new technological innovations, changing the rules of public service reform rather than just playing the game more effectively.

In this essay we describe the role of technology in delivering different forms of innovation and set out the kinds of ecosystem that government must create if it wants to realise the full benefit of the digital era.

Innovation for productivity and efficiency

The public sector is encouraging and using new technology solutions to improve efficiency and productivity. Indeed, technology was seen as a major enabler of efficiency in Peter Gershon's report.[2] Gershon's attempt to apply private sector best practice is not now seen as particularly innovative – but it is important to remember that these practices had never before been used in the uniquely large and complex public sector environment.

Hewlett-Packard (HP) worked with the government officials shaping the strategy for these efficiency programmes, using the experience of the HP–Compaq merger – the largest IT merger in corporate history – to help establish the approach required to join up large-scale and complex IT and administrative systems. In doing so, we laid the basis for major efficiency savings through better knowledge management and shared service approaches.

It should be remembered that joining up back-office systems can deliver far more than simple efficiencies. If implemented in the right way, these changes can enable innovation in the provision and delivery of public services, making them more responsive and customer-focused.

The Worcestershire Hub

An example of shared services leading to innovative service delivery is the Worcestershire Hub. The project grew out of the Worcestershire Local Strategic Partnership in the late 1990s and has been taken forward by the Worcestershire e-Government Partnership, which comprises Worcestershire County Council, the local District Councils and other public service partners, such as the Fire Service and the Police. The Hub provides citizens with a single point of contact for all District and County Council services as well as those of partner organisations.

Rather than simply creating a single call centre for all enquiries, the Worcestershire partners have created a network of local service centres open to the public for face-to-face visits, but which also act as a virtual call centre and handle enquiries coming through the Hub's website. Whichever method of contact is chosen, the customer advisers can access the same customer relationship software that holds records of previous enquiries from individuals and allows a seamless service whomever the customer is talking to.

While the technology may not be new, the joined-up approach taken in Worcestershire was innovative because for the first time it allowed services that previously required multiple phone calls during office hours to be provided 24 hours a day, seven days a week via the Hub's website. As well as a point of contact for general enquiries, visitors to the website can report abandoned vehicles, problems with street lighting or simply renew a library book. The system has also enabled a better service to be delivered with 80 per cent of enquiries now being resolved at the first point of contact and customer satisfaction ratings of 95 per cent. At the same time, the project has saved the project partners around £14 million per year.

Making services more responsive to the citizen

Public service innovation is also driven by policy changes designed to improve the effectiveness of service outcomes and make services more responsive to the citizen. One such policy is the personalisation agenda, which again seeks to mirror innovation in private sector services. Personalisation in the private sector has been enabled by the development of technology that can track the specific requirements and interests of an individual customer and tailor services to their needs.

Education has been at the forefront of the drive for personalisation in the public sector; however, the requirement for a national education infrastructure on which to build personalised learning has proved a significant challenge. This has not been the case, however, in Northern Ireland, where the province's 1200 schools provide enough scale to make a common infrastructure work without it becoming unwieldy.

Classroom 2000

Northern Ireland has used technology to underpin the personalised delivery of education services. Its Classroom 2000 (C2K) project is built on a network that connects all of the province's 1245 schools to a central data centre in Belfast.

With over 375,000 pupils and teachers using the system, C2K is one of the world's largest education technology projects and has delivered many benefits to Northern Ireland. Pupils now have access to secure email and the internet from their first day at primary school and so are growing up with the vital IT skills that are needed in today's economy. As well as being able to communicate and work with other pupils across the province via email, text or video conferencing, C2K also provides them with access to a wide range of digital material that helps them with their school work.

Some of this material comes from their own schools, some is supplied centrally by the C2K project and some is accessible from sources such as the BBC and online libraries. Specialist subject teachers in a particular school are also able to deliver lessons to pupils across a number of different schools, so widening the subject choice and providing greater personalisation of the curriculum.

For teachers, C2K provides the ability to access a range of teaching materials from across the world as well as a forum for sharing ideas and best practice. They are also able to monitor pupils' progress more effectively and to deliver lessons to pupils online so they can catch up out of school hours. The C2K project also allows parents to become more involved in their children's education. Parents are able to access the system securely from their home, local library or anywhere else that has internet access. This allows parents to see what their child's homework is, and what resources are available to help them. They can also check how their child is progressing at school by looking at online assessments. In addition, C2K is now being extended for use in adult education, allowing members of the community to access learning material via their home PC, local libraries or community centre.

Innovation arising from technological development

As set out above, the National Audit Office identified two types of innovation: innovation aimed at increasing productivity and efficiency and innovation aimed at making services more responsive to the citizen. From HP's experience of working and innovating in the UK private and public sectors, we would add a third type of public sector innovation to this list: innovation that arises from disruptive technologies that have the ability to significantly change the model of public service delivery.

Disruptive technologies are those that fundamentally change the way things are done, radically improving existing approaches, or creating entirely new markets. Mobile telephony and email are recent examples. It is hardly surprising that these technologies rarely impact on the public sector as quickly as they do on the private.

In general, government cannot afford financially or politically to experiment with unproven technologies. This means that the lag time between the emergence of a technology and its adoption by the public sector can be considerable. Even when the technology is adopted, there are severe risks of misunderstanding its potential application. The sheer scale of government institutions can lead to over-ambition – good technology easily gets lost in the complexity of implementing huge schemes. From a different perspective, when politicians adopt web 2.0 technologies – for instance the Labour and Conservative parties' experiments with YouTube and Webcameron – they risk derision for 'jumping on the bandwagon' rather than being seen as truly embracing collaborative and user-focused innovation.

'Innovative ecosystems'

While it may be a general rule that the public sector does not get involved in disruptive technologies (until they are firmly established), there is space to create partnerships between the public and private sectors to develop small-scale trials of innovative approaches that utilise cutting-edge technology. The private sector can provide ideas and technology, but it often needs access to imaginative public sector organisations and public service users to understand how disruptive technologies will work in context. By finding out what works for service providers and their users, these partnerships can help to manage the risks associated with disruptive technology and open up a new field of innovation to the public sector.

HP is developing a range of these partnerships to identify the likely impact of four major trends that are emerging in the technology sector:

1   convergence of communication and computing –
    computing services being delivered as a service across the
    communication infrastructure, with powerful
    applications available on a wide range of communication
    platforms
2   commoditisation of technology as the price is driven
    down and performance increases
3   virtualised computing in which the emphasis is less on
    powerful machines, and more on creating centralised
    servers and storage facilities that can be accessed by a wide
    range of small, personal devices
4   utility computing – where powerful computing services
    are available by subscription and users are charged only
    for the amount of the service they actually use, avoiding
    the need to build in 'redundancy' to IT systems.

While each of these four developing areas offers a platform for significant innovation in public service delivery, government is not able to take on the risk of developing these innovative services alone. So, in their work with academics and a range of public sector partners, HP researchers have developed what have been termed 'innovation ecosystems', where partners in a research project each gain an insight into innovation in their own area of interest.

Pervasive computing

These four trends clear the way for an exciting new era of techno-logical development. *Pervasive computing* offers new possibilities for public service reform, and it is an example of one key area where HP has been developing innovation ecosystems.

Pervasive computing involves the integration of computing and communications technology into everyday items to create an environment where these items are wirelessly integrated. The concept behind such integration is that it will allow users to interact more naturally and casually with their environment. A completely pervasive computing environment is some way off, but as computing technology becomes truly mobile there is an emerging market in devices such as wearable computers and automated 'smart homes', which may form the building blocks of a pervasive computing environment.

Pervasive computing is not based on the development of new technologies but an innovative use of existing technologies, such as mobile phone technology, voice recognition systems, radio-frequency identification (RFID) tags and smart cards. While there is considerable uncertainty within the technology sector regarding the future of this technology, it is clear that there are potential applications in a variety of areas including health and education. The problem is how to develop a technology that achieves its potential in terms of delivering value to customers.

One of the core principles in creating new technology approaches is the principle of 'next bench experience' – or the idea that one innovation will build on another and then tend to lead to the next innovation. In December 2005 HP tried to set this kind of development in motion. The company made available, free of charge, a pervasive computing toolkit that provided other developers with the basic tools needed to develop their own applications. A group at Nottingham University took up this challenge and developed an application using biosensors that introduced children to the idea that they could improve their health by measuring and monitoring their heart rate. Using the toolkit they developed a game that encouraged children to exercise.

This collaborative approach to innovation implicitly recognises that in order to be innovative, to truly reveal the new rules of the game, an ecosystem of innovators, developers and users is required if innovation is to deliver on its full potential.

Mobile Bristol 'mediascapes'

A further example of the development of an innovation ecosystem is HP's work to develop 'mediascapes', as part of a Department of Trade and Industry funded project with Bristol University called 'Mobile Bristol'. The project uses HP technology to create digital landscapes that overlay the physical world to create a mobile virtual reality. By walking around the landscape, users can experience digitised sights and sounds activated by their movement.

The Mobile Bristol team has created a series of innovation ecosystems of business, academic research, technologists, media producers, artists, educationalists and local communities to develop the mediascapes. These new platforms have enabled this multi-skilled community to explore new media, new business opportunities and new ways to interact with the physical environment. The education sector has been one of the first beneficiaries of the project with students from one local school invited to participate in a mediascape of an African savannah.

Students were able to experience life as a pride of lions in two related arenas of activity. In the first, children have to survive 'as lions' outside on a playing field, interacting with a virtual savannah and exploring the opportunities and risks to lions in that space. Children are given HP iPAQs, multimedia handheld devices linked to satellite positioning systems. Through these devices they 'see', 'hear' and 'smell' the world of the savannah as they navigate the real space outdoors as a pride of lions. The second domain, the 'den', is an indoor space where children can plan, research and reflect on their outdoor game-play through accessing resources such as the internet, books, adult experts and an interface that has tracked their outdoor activities.

The project – known as Savannah – has identified that the main motivating feature of games is not complex graphics, but the establishment of appropriate and authentic challenges. Alongside this, the trials have demonstrated that in order for games technologies to prove effective in education, there is a need to develop new learning environments in which children are given high degrees of control over how they manage their time and their information resources. Collaboration between the Mobile Bristol team and the National Endowment for Science, Technology and the Arts (NESTA) has now led to a project to deliver a 'Mediascape Building Toolkit' to all the schools in the UK.

Once again, this project demonstrates how leading-edge technological innovation is often the product of partnerships between public bodies and highly skilled specialist organisations from the private sector. For the public sector, these partnerships can take the risk out of experimenting with new forms of public service delivery and to identify the possibilities of user-focused innovations.

Conclusion

While it may seem counterintuitive, cutting-edge technological innovation does have a role to play in developing innovative public services, but this level of innovation has to be developed within an ecosystem encompassing the private sector, academia and a wide range of stakeholders in order to allow for trial and error without significant risk to the public service provider. This role for technological innovation in the public sector sits alongside the established role technology has in improving organisational efficiency and the role that a robust technology infrastructure plays in delivering innovative personalised services.

We believe that harnessing all three of these models of innovation will help us move beyond the two extremes of either unfettered increases in public spending or unrelenting efficiency drives in order to allow the public sector to invest in the best tools to meet the challenge of delivering better public services in the twenty-first century. By using the right approach to innovation and the right approach to technology we can develop new approaches that are simultaneously more efficient and more effective.

Rob Watt is Public Sector Business Development Director, HP.

Notes

1   National Audit Office, *Achieving Innovation in Central Government Organisations* (London: TSO, Jul 2006), available at www.nao.org.uk/ publications/nao_reports/05-06/05061447i.pdf (accessed 12 Jun 2007).
2   P Gershon, *Releasing Resources for the Frontline* (London: HM Treasury, 2004).

10. Transforming government

David Varney

Our economy is changing rapidly and will continue to do so in coming years. The UK is moving away from the traditional industries that defined it, with manufacturing now accounting for a mere 16 per cent of gross GDP. In the future, our wealth as a country will rest with the service industries (72 per cent of GDP), the creative industries and those areas of manufacturing such as biotechnology in which the edge comes from innovation rather than price. These transitions are taking place in the context of an increasingly competitive world, in which heavy skills investment by China and India is starting to challenge ever larger swathes of the UK workforce.

The service sector is essential to our economic vitality, so we all have an interest in its productivity and innovative capacity. This is particularly true in the case of public services, which absorb 20 per cent of GDP – a figure likely to grow in the future. This means that we cannot be satisfied with simply creating a productive private sector. We should also be thoroughly investigating public services as sites of innovation, improved productivity and skills development.

Cutting-edge technological advances are becoming perhaps the single most important factor in transforming our service sectors. Businesses are using technology to revolutionise the contact that they have with customers, providing service that is more bespoke, at any hour of the day, which is rapid, responsive and can be accessed without ever having to leave the house. Sadly, it is the case that public services often lag behind the most advanced of businesses in how they are using technology to transform contact and connections between users and organisations.

In recent years, we have seen a number of initiatives focused on increasing efficiency and productivity in our public services. Most of these have concentrated on 'back office' administrative tasks. Business process redesign and shared services agendas have been the main tools of change, and there has been relatively little focus on the 'front end' of services. The interactions between services and people's lives have been relatively neglected.

My argument in this essay is that, through the innovative application of technology to this neglected 'front end' of services, we can create greater efficiencies *and* improved service experiences.

Disconnected service

But first, let us assess the scale of the challenge implied by a transformation of contact between people and services. Over the course of the review I led for HM Treasury in 2006,[1] my team and I uncovered a series of examples of people's experiences of contact with government in a range of settings. These serve to illustrate the scale of the change necessary:

○ There are 61 different benefits entitlements forms – the majority of which require the same standard information to be provided by benefit applicants. In most cases, links between the different benefit entitlements are not being made, meaning that some people may be missing entitlements that they are due.

○ Within a year, an average citizen will need to prove their identity to government at least 11 times.

○ A small business recruiting a new member of staff has to comply with a range of regulations. Currently if this business seeks guidance from government, it will be faced with over 20 helplines, and links to more than 25 additional websites.

O   Perhaps most starkly, a 2005 Cabinet Office report[2] presented an example of what one typical family had to go through following a bereavement. After the person died in an accident in September 2004, the family had a total of 44 contacts with government over the following 180 days. Even after that time, there were still unresolved issues around the deceased man's passport, and queries about housing benefit.

Government delivers services through departments, which might deliver the service directly, through agencies or agents, alone or in cooperation with local government. Each solution that is developed is a child of its time and circumstances, and the end result is that citizens with multiple needs are left to join up the various islands of service to meet those needs. Inevitably, the most vulnerable groups in society are those which suffer the most from this fragmented government landscape; they have the most complex needs, as well as often having the least capacity to navigate the confusing array of helplines, call centres, websites and frontline offices that are on offer. The burden of accessing the right government service, armed with the right information, proof of identity and so on, is so high that they may not get what they need.

Customer or citizen?

The history of public services has led to departments or agencies focusing on the supply of specific products, rather than taking a citizen- or business-led approach. This has led to departments often focusing not on the whole citizen, but instead on a particular aspect of that citizen that they call the 'customer'. So, for example, a lone, unemployed parent might be a benefit claimant to one department, a parent to another, a patient to another and a learner to another. By seeing this parent as a customer, each department can focus on the delivery of its own particular service, often failing to see the way that its offering interacts with those of other departments and services.

Customer focus works well for private providers in competitive markets, where providers need to understand and influence customer choices. Businesses 'segment' their customers – targeting particular people or groups of people who will be interested in purchasing their specific products or services. There is a lot that can be learnt from this work and indeed many public service organisations are increasingly talking of 'customer focus' as their driving mission.

However, within public services, 'the customer' is often taken to mean the individual who receives a particular benefit or entitlement, rather than considering the needs of the individual as a whole. This is profoundly at odds with how people themselves relate to public services. Often they are trying to deal with a task or an event that does not fall neatly or obviously within any one part of government – for example, getting married, losing your job, starting a business, or dealing with a bereavement.

Nevertheless, it is certainly true that our expectations of service experiences are rising fast in response to the seamless, 24/7 services we often receive from commercial businesses. Regardless of whether we see ourselves as customers or citizens, we expect our problem to be resolved the first time round, intruding on our time as little as possible. We want convenience and value for money.

Over the next ten years, government has an opportunity to provide better public services for citizens and businesses, and to do so at a lower cost to taxpayers. The key to doing this lies in the way we invest in and deploy new technology. The remainder of this essay notes three core dimensions of an agenda for action.

A single point of contact for citizens and businesses

Citizens should have a single point of contact with government to meet a range of their needs, and businesses should have to provide information only once.

Achieving this aspiration requires a much more effective grouping of public service delivery around common themes that are meaningful for citizens and businesses. My review of the government's strategy for using different communication channels recommended that such an approach should be piloted, initially through exploring what a single point of contact might look like for the changes in circumstances associated with bereavement, birth and change of address. The work is now being taken forward by the Department for Work and Pensions and HM Revenue and Customs (HMRC) jointly, and its findings will provide the basis for a methodology to transform public service delivery.

There is much to learn from other initiatives around the world that have experimented with new approaches to contact management. For example, the Canadian government has launched Service Canada, providing a one-stop-shop facility to contact central government services. New Brunswick provides multi-channel one-stop shopping for government services for its residents. Denmark has introduced a one-stop change of address service. New York City and others have introduced a single number to access government services. Finally, Belgium has introduced legislation to provide information that means citizens provide information only once to government, forcing departments and agencies to do the joining up.

Of course, there are excellent examples around the UK of public sector organisations cooperating in order to give citizens and businesses a better service. But more fundamental and widespread change is necessary if the public sector economy is to match the performance of the best service providers.

A channel optimisation strategy

In the early days of e-government, there was occasionally a sense that real transformation would come from transferring all services to the virtual world. This approach is misleading. The government's strategy for investment in technology and new forms of contact with citizens must instead be led by a focus on channel *optimisation* – matching each channel, whether phone, internet or face-to-face contact, to its best use for particular citizens.

Experience from the use of Directgov and Businesslink.gov.uk demonstrates the clear benefits (to both users and the public sector) of increasing the appropriate use of e-services. E-channels, when properly developed, can offer joined-up information and transactional services. Creating effective online provision will lead to people choosing this channel as a first point of contact, representing significant savings for government. Contact centres enable the resolution of more complex issues that cannot be dealt with by an e-channel.

Of course, there will always be a need for essential face-to-face contact. However, the amount of face-to-face contact should decrease as other contact channels become more effective – thereby enabling more effective targeting of resources to those most in need of support.

By dealing more efficiently with routine transactions and by reducing the complexity of having to deal with different parts of government in different ways, service providers will be able to devote more time to delivering a personalised service to individuals. This may involve less time spent on carrying out routine identity and entitlement checks, and more time on resolving complex problems or helping people access services where they are having difficulty.

A deep understanding of channel optimisation will grow only out of much smarter, more systematic use of citizen and business insight data. The essay in this collection by Chris Naylor highlights how powerful such approaches can be when applied at the level of the whole organisation rather than in a more piecemeal, project-by-project approach.

A strategic approach to identity management

A joined-up identity management regime is the foundation of service transformation. The ultimate aim should be a common registration system – from birth to death, immigration to emigration. This would simplify life for individuals by ensuring a consistent set of information across government, which is carried over and expanded as later life events or the need for new services occur.

Peter Gershon identified £21.5 billion of efficiency savings to be released by 2007/08,[3] primarily through improved procurement, shared services and business process redesign. There remain significant opportunities for improvement across all of these;

however, there are also opportunities to create efficiencies through joining up frontline services, resolving customer inquiries at the first contact, and designing contacts around the needs of the citizen or business.

Duplication continues to be a major source of inefficiency – for example, numerous government databases hold the same address information, all requiring separate input. We have multiple identity management systems carrying out the same functions. In HMRC alone, it is estimated that £100 million savings a year can come from better record management, eradicating duplication of effort and improving the quality of information.

By its very nature, identity is a personal and sensitive issue. The systems we create for managing identity in government must acknowledge this sensitivity and respect a person's right to privacy. However, at the moment there are approximately 300 million contact details in the public sector – almost five sets of information for every citizen.[4]

Once again, we cannot be under any illusions about the scale of the challenge implied by this. The Home Office has 20 verification procedures and 25 unique personal numbers. For tax and benefits there are ten initiatives each using a unique number, and in children's services there are nine. And locally, there are over 400 local councils, delivering 670 services through 4000 types of transaction.

Conclusion

The true customer contact innovations from technology will emerge only if this is a *corporate* agenda that cuts across pre-existing government departments, silos, agencies and delivery organisations. The best innovations will be those that use new channels to create genuinely new approaches to service delivery; these will be new approaches that are not simply the transposition of the same, piecemeal offering from one channel to another, but instead represent an entirely new form of contact and dialogue between citizens and service providers.

The evolution of the e-channel and its use by the private sector has been fast-paced, with the most successful organisations moving from providing simple informational sites to transactional services, supported by search engines to enable people to navigate an ever-growing maze of information. The development of web 2.0 is beginning to herald yet another shift, from transactional to interactional websites, where contributions by citizens and businesses are integral to the content and development of both the site and the service, and where citizen contributions enable organisations to offer back to them increasingly personalised support.

The challenge now for government is to embrace not only today's technology, but also tomorrow's, and to ensure that it deploys that technology in a way that is driven by enhancing the contact and interactions between people and services. It is through this enhancement that we stand a chance of achieving our twin aspirations of better *and* more productive services. That can only be a good thing, for each of us as citizens, and for our economy as a whole.

David Varney is HM Treasury adviser of transformational government.

Notes

1   Cabinet Office, *Transformational Government: Enabled by technology*, Cm 6683 (Norwich TSO, 2006), available at www.cio.gov.uk/documents/pdf/ transgov/transgov-strategy.pdf (accessed 18 Jun 2007).
2   Cabinet Office, *Making a Difference: Bereavement* (London: Cabinet Office, 2005).
3   P Gershon, *Releasing Resources for the Frontline* (London: HM Treasury, 2004).
4   See 'Better sharing of citizen data across the public sector', Citizen Information Project, 2005, available at www.gro.gov.uk/cip (accessed 27 Jun 2007).

Systems of governing

11. Porous government

Co-design as a route to innovation
Sophia Parker

The idea of involving the public as designers of their own services is already being seen as a key element of the next wave of public service reform. Much hope is being invested in the idea that user-driven change will lead to better services, improved outcomes and greater legitimacy for state action. Less, however, is said by governments about co-design as a source of *innovation*. While most departments have signed up to the principle that co-design processes can make existing services better, there are far fewer examples of governments embracing co-design processes as part of a broader innovation strategy.

Despite the warm words of recent policy initiatives, it seems that co-design is rather like spinach: governments know it is good for them, but they don't always like it. This essay explores some principles that, taken together, could represent the embedding of co-design not only in processes of improvement, but also in approaches to innovation at a systemic level. I draw on user-driven innovation literature, as well as emerging practice in this field.

User-driven innovation is hardly a new phenomenon; what is new is the necessary shift in *mindset* about how strategy is developed and how innovation is nurtured. Investing systematically in user-driven innovation in the public sector has huge implications for models of management and for the processes by which policy is developed and implemented.

Government will need to become more porous, letting people into previously closed systems of policy-making. It may feel counterintuitive to those sitting in Whitehall offices, but in order to gain legitimacy they will need to be willing to give up more power to the public and to let service users into policy development cycles at much earlier stages.

If an agenda based on co-design and user-driven innovation is to work, then the shift in power has to be real. As evidenced by attitudes to the perceived 'consultation overdrive' since 1997, people are quick to recognise an empty promise of greater power, where consultation has little real impact on final decisions, and where bottom-up deliberation continues to be trumped by top-down directives.

Nevertheless, there are occasional moments in time when a number of agendas come together and produce an opportunity for a genuine shift in how the business of government is carried out. Often these moments are not the 'lightning bolt' they appear to be after the event. Instead, they emerge out of the entrepreneurial connecting together of a series of possibilities, a combination of inspiration and perspiration in the quest to bring about improvement, change and transformation.

The next section outlines three related shifts – a changing economy, a new understanding of innovation, and altered expectations of what the state is for – that I believe could create fertile ground for a unique user-driven innovation agenda in the UK public sector. If there is one concept that could be the central value underpinning such an agenda, it is co-design.

The convergence of three trends

When it comes to innovation policy, services are the poor relation of manufacturing and technological development, with much of the focus having been on how government can invest in scientific R&D, the development of a supportive intellectual property and patenting system, and a series of tax breaks and other benefits to incubate new businesses.[1]

Yet this framework for investing in innovation is increasingly outdated for the UK's burgeoning service economy. Earlier in 2007, the percentage of GDP generated by service industries increased to 74.8 per cent. Over the next 20 years, as changes in our demographic profile and lifestyles bite, public services will represent a growing proportion of this figure, as health, education and care begin to overtake the automotive and financial service sectors in terms of their impact on the economic prosperity of the country. Creating an innovation framework that invests in public services as systematically as it does in more traditional areas of R&D will become an imperative.

If the first driver is a changing economy, the second is a changing understanding of what innovation is and how it happens. Two archetypes of innovation processes continue to guide policy in this area: one, an entrepreneur-led model where innovations are seen to emerge from the inventions and ideas of geeks and boffins; and two, a technology-led model where new hardware creates the disruption necessary for radical innovation.

A new archetype is emerging in the fields of product design and software development: that of the user as innovator. In these fields, academics such as Eric von Hippel[2] and CK Prahalad[3] have argued that innovation requires user knowledge as much as it needs new forms of technology or eureka moments. Much less work has been done on this archetype and what it might look like in the context of services, but at its most simple it would mean that users must be recognised and valued as major sources of innovation, rather than simply being seen as passive consumers of fixed chunks of service.

The gathering momentum behind user-driven innovation connects directly to the third trend of relevance here: a shift in our understanding of the relationship between the state and its citizenry. No longer content with a deficit model of services that remedies only our most pressing problems, we increasingly demand a social investment state: as well as small class sizes we want lifelong learners; as well as clean hospitals we want long, healthy lives; as well as excellent residential care, we want independence and dignity.

Such a shift in emphasis means that it is impossible to conceive of a public service agenda without taking account of the role of the citizen as much as the role of the state. For example, lifelong learners cannot be 'delivered' by an efficient machine – the policy objective relies on engaging people, tapping into and then supporting their desire to learn continuously. The broad acceptance across parties of the notions of 'co-production' and 'co-design' – in rhetoric at least – indicates that this is an agenda that is not going to go away.

These trends create the opportunity for a new, ambitious and inspiring story about public service reform and transformation: a chance to imagine what it might look like if government understood people's own experiences and lives as potential sites of learning and innovation.

Co-design 1.0: valuing new forms of evidence

The emerging user-driven innovation paradigm has grown from a recognition that two forms of knowledge are necessary to develop a new product or service. These are, first, usage and context-of-usage insight – understanding needs and the ways people will use a product or service – and, second, solutions know-how. Traditionally, firms have relied on market research and related disciplines to understand what users need and want. Von Hippel and others argued that this was not a powerful, accurate or efficient way of gathering such insight – and on the basis of this belief, his thesis about user involvement was born.

But von Hippel's work has yet to permeate Whitehall. It is nearly one hundred years since Schumpeter wrote of firms as the primary agents of product development and economic progress, and yet many of our business models and value systems continue to be coloured by his manufacturing-centric worldview where organisations are the primary engines for innovation. This means that, typically, governments privilege some forms of knowledge – system-level, producer-focused, quantitative data – over user-based experiential evidence. Or in von Hippel's words, they prefer solutions know-how to user and usage insights.

The shift from Schumpeter to von Hippel has two key implications for a public sector innovation strategy.

First, policy-makers would have to focus on creating greater parity between different forms of evidence and insight. That would mean developing greater capacity within government to gather user and usage evidence. This isn't simply about consulting more: the process of insight generation and user participation is a skilled one. For example, leading 'empathic design' firm IDEO uses over 50 different methodologies to help it uncover and understand not only user needs and wants, but also their tacit and latent desires. These methods are vital: as Henry Ford once said, if he had just asked people what they wanted, he would have focused on how to make horses go faster.

Second, such a strategy would have to consider how to bring together a range of different people to redesign a service. Co-design is about making users equal partners in a collective process, rather than giving them precedence over other players. Creating multi-disciplinary teams of people who have different perspectives on the same problem, and investing time in helping those team members to recognise the validity of alternative points of view, increases the chances of generating radical new ideas that have a good chance of working in practice.

Co-design 2.0: principles for porous government

Co-design means we have to value different kinds of people and evidence in the policy-making process, but it is only a starting point. In isolation this approach is little more than tinkering with existing approaches to policy development. It simply demands that government find some new tools and methods to engage users in a process that is still fundamentally 'owned' and mediated by public service professionals and policy-makers. The risk is that, on its own, this understanding of co-design would become little more than a sophisticated approach to consultation.

There remains much to be done to understand how the tools and techniques of co-design can be better used at the level of specific services, where, for example, hospitals might work with patients and former patients to improve their experiences.

But emerging practice in both the public sector and elsewhere hints at a much more radical interpretation of co-design, where it is used as a means of innovating at the level of whole *systems* of services. The three principles I outline in the remainder of this essay demonstrate how government could adopt co-design not only to 'let people in' to existing policy processes, but also to take policy development out into the field. Users have a part to play in more disruptive innovations, as well as the processes of continuous improvement.

1. Seek out and nurture the rule-breakers

A user-driven innovation strategy would not seek to work with all users, all of the time. Von Hippel estimated that between 10 per cent and 40 per cent of people are likely to be involved in developing or modifying products.[4] A similar estimate for the NHS put this figure at approximately 20 per cent.[5] These estimates are an important reminder that users are not all inherently innovative.

Nor would such a strategy define users as exclusively 'end users' or 'consumers'. Service interactions usually involve both a practitioner and a user, both of whom rely on broader policy frameworks. Effective policy has to recognise the needs of both groups equally.

Government therefore needs to move beyond general assertions about user engagement and focus instead on a smaller group of 'lead users' – the 'positive deviants' – the maverick producers and users who push the system to do things it was not designed to do. Policy-makers need to proactively seek out these people, and then nurture their work through connecting them to others and providing resources of support.

The BBC Innovation Labs programme offers some powerful insights into how this might work.[6] The corporation has developed a set of online tools that allows it to identify groups of 'lead users' in areas of particular interest. Having identified these people, the BBC then supports and incubates their ideas through a week-long 'lab' based on conversation, ideas exchange, mentor support from experts in user-centred design, and challenge from the BBC commissioners themselves. Some of the ideas are then taken into further development mode by the BBC; some go no further but at the very least, Lab participants have met a new network and have been paid for their time and contributions.

Simon Duffy's essay on the genesis of in Control hints at what this approach might look like in the context of the public sector. One way of understanding in Control is to see it as a network of rule breakers, redesigning the social care system through a constant and iterative process of 'versioning' and reflection. At the core of their approach is constant scanning for those people inventing new ways of doing things, in order to support and learn from their approaches. Their work could ultimately redesign the entire system of social care at the same time as turning the policy development and service innovation process inside out.

2. Give people tools, not ideas

Three years ago, Demos, the service design consultancy Engine and the Department for Education and Skills Innovation Unit developed a strategy to 'roll out' the commitment to personalised learning outlined by the then Minister for Schools, David Miliband. The traditional approach would have been to set up a programme board, devise a performance management framework and some formal guidance to instruct schools in how they needed to change their practice.

Instead, we developed a toolkit for teachers.[7] Designed in collaboration with a small group of 'rule-breaking' heads, we created a resource designed to connect the personalisation agenda with the individual contexts of each school – enabling those schools to build on work they were already proud of, and providing them with exercises to help them reflect on what personalised learning might look and feel like in practice.

The initial evaluation was powerful: the toolkits were massively popular, and made a real difference to practice and priorities in schools up and down the country. What was different in our approach is that we created *tools* to give people the time, space and confidence to unlock and explore their own ideas, rather than telling people what to do, or seeking to create a blueprint that then required implementation.

A strategy for user-driven innovation would not seek to feed people ideas, but instead to provide them with tools. This is about fostering a permeable development culture – a significant shift away from more traditional approaches, which have focused on identifying and codifying 'best practice' before attempting to spread it around the system via legislation, regulation and inspection – a strategy characterised by some as 'the tyranny of best practice'.

In other words, toolkits are a simple, cost-effective and efficient way of uncovering and understanding user needs. They enable innovation to bubble up anywhere, and they can also harness the power of 'accidental discovery' – like text messaging, those innovations that emerge when someone is trying to do something else.

Companies like Electronic Arts, creators of the massively popular SIMS computer game, have built on this insight and now offer a range of toolkits that people can use to create their own virtual environments or develop new items to use in the game. The toolkits range from the very basic to the highly advanced, that people can use as their confidence increases.

3. Create 'in between spaces' for R&D activity

Proctor and Gamble employs 7500 scientists, but through its InnovCentive network, it draws on the knowledge of a further 90,000 scientists and researchers in its R&D processes. Investing in this network beyond the fixed boundaries of the organisation is central to its success in developing better and new products. Far from threatening a firm's position, giving away knowledge and opening up previously closed processes can enable companies to maintain their market position and to continuously innovate.

Similarly, when the Prudential created the online bank Egg, it told the lead developer, Richard Duvall, to remove himself from the constraints of the day-to-day operations of the major bank. The Pru recognised that 'the way we do things here' can be a major limit on the extent to which radical innovations or new service models might emerge, and so gave Richard complete freedom to re-imagine the service and all its dimensions.

Both of these stories point to the fact that while it is imperative that overall innovative capacity of the public sector is enhanced, some more radical forms of innovation need to be incubated and supported in a separate space not constrained by institutional parameters and functional boundaries. Too much questioning of 'the fundamentals' can be disruptive and disorienting in organisations under enormous pressure to continue to deliver excellent and efficient services on a daily basis.

This suggests that existing institutions may not always be able to navigate the tension between the pressing need for innovation and the danger that innovative processes lead to unacceptable disruption. So government innovation strategies need to outline how the public sector might invest in new spaces 'in-between' existing bodies. There are some examples of organisations that have interpreted this very literally, creating labs or neutral spaces for radical innovation work to take place in. Mette Abrahamsen's essay on MindLab is one such example of this. In the UK, the impressive Solution Centre is a core part of the Pensions Service at Department for Work and Pensions. Kent County Council is piloting a similar approach.

There is some evidence to support the idea that neutral, safe spaces are important contributors to the innovation process and outcomes; however, as a bare minimum, these 'in between' spaces need to be about *permission* – permission to question everything in the quest for new ideas and solutions that might work.

Co-design for life

Adopting the principles outlined here would certainly unlock a wave of innovation in public services, but it would also be extremely challenging for government. While much has been made of the changing role of *users* in the innovation process, less has been said about the need to shift the activities and mindsets of those working *within* the bureaucracy.

Co-design is not the easy option, pushing ever greater responsibility for problem-solving on to users. It is not about government doing less. Rather, it is about government operating differently, more collaboratively and openly with citizens. This form of collaboration takes time, effort and know-how. It takes a willingness to recognise new forms of knowledge in the innovation process. But most importantly it requires a commitment to sharing power with users, practitioners and others to play an active role in developing whole systems of services.

There are many indications that government is moving in the right direction – take for example the recent policy review, which modelled a deliberative and open approach to the development of recommendations. But this kind of work is just the tip of the iceberg.

If co-design is to become a route to real innovation, then we must examine the extent to which government believes it can devise and implement change and innovation in isolation from users and citizens. Degrees of success in co-design approaches – the policy review, the expert patients programme, in Control pilots – should provide impetus to a set of public sector institutions still clouded by a legacy of scientific, rational theories of the organisation where users are not seen to have anything other than needs.

In this context, the challenge for policy-makers is to build upwards and outwards from these pockets of success, rather than seeking to push back on the innovations such approaches have generated through the instinctive desire to legislate, regulate and control.

If the evidence is there in terms of 'proofs of concept', then the government has the opportunity to bring together the three trends outlined earlier in this essay, and connect them to a far more radical and ambitious agenda for public service reform and transformation. The question remains whether the UK's centralised governing institutions can ever really adopt a new model of change in which transformation grows from the imagination and participation of practitioners, users and citizens, and where government energies are spent less on codifying practice and pushing ideas out from the centre, and more on finding new ways of tapping into the motivations, energies and ideas of user–innovators around the system. It is only through addressing this that co-design's full potential as a source of innovation will be released.

Sophia Parker is a Demos associate and is co-director of designedbyus.

Notes

1   NESTA, *The Innovation Gap: Why policy needs to reflect the reality of innovation in the UK* (London: National Endowment for Science, Technology and the Arts, 2006), available at www.nesta.org.uk/assets/pdf/innovation_gap_report_NESTA.pdf (accessed 18 June 2007).

2   E von Hippel, *Democratising Innovation* (Cambridge, MA, and London: MIT Press, 2005), available at http://web.mit.edu/evhippel/www/democ1.htm (accessed 18 Jun 2007).

3   CK Prahalad, *The Fortune at the Bottom of the Pyramid: Eradicating poverty through profits* (Philadelphia, PA: Wharton School Publishing, 2004).

4   von Hippel, *Democratising Innovation*.

5   P Bate, H Bevan and G Robert, *Towards a Million Change Agents: A review of the social movement literature; implications for large scale change in the NHS* (London: NHS Modernisation Agency, 2004), see www.institute.nhs.uk/building_capability/new_methods%2c_tools_and_appro aches_.../social_movements.html (accessed 20 Jun 2007).

6   See http://open.bbc.co.uk/labs/ (accessed 20 Jun 2007).

7   'Picture This! Planning for personalization', available at www.innovation-unit.co.uk/media/publications/picture-this.html (accessed 18 Jun 2007).

12. Scaling up innovation

The ultimate challenge
Geoff Mulgan and Simon Tucker

Governments across the world face electorates with rising aspirations: they expect ever better public services, more fitted to their needs, and more easily accessible. They also expect governments to keep up with changing priorities – ageing populations, the rising incidence of chronic disease, climate change – and to do better at resolving long-standing problems like stubbornly persistent rates of youth disengagement and alienation.

None of these challenges can be solved by continuing with business as usual. Nor will they be dealt with by efficiency drives and incremental improvement. Hence the growing interest in more systematic approaches to innovation in the public sector, particularly in those countries which do best in terms of day-to-day performance – like Denmark, Canada, Finland and Singapore.

Public innovation can come in many different guises – from new ways of organising things (like public–private partnerships) to new ways of rewarding people (like performance-related pay) and new ways of communicating (like ministerial blogs). Distinctions are sometimes made between policy innovations, service innovations and innovations in other fields like democracy (e-voting, citizens' juries). Some innovations are so radical that they warrant being seen as systemic (like the creation of a national health service or the move to a low-carbon economy).

Governments and public agencies around the world are constantly innovating new ways of organising social security or healthcare, online portals and smart cards, public health programmes and imaginative incentives to cut carbon emissions. Some of the more prominent recent examples in the UK would include NHS Direct and learndirect; drug courts and police community support officers; online tax transactions and restorative justice; cognitive behavioural therapy for prisoners and Sure Start; Connexions and criminal assets recovery; congestion charges and children's commissioners.

Alongside new organisations and programmes, the public sector has also innovated what Bart Nooteboom calls new 'scripts'.[1] An example from the private sector was the rise of fast-food retailing, which created a new script for having a meal. Where the traditional restaurant script was choose, be served, eat, then pay, the self-service/fast-food script is choose, pay, carry food to table, eat, clear up. New scripts are emerging right across the public sector, in areas like recycling, personalised learning in schools and self-managed healthcare – and are likely to be critical to future productivity gains in public services.

On the face of it, scaling up these inventions from good local ideas to widely accepted practices should not be an inherent problem for governments, which possess the power, money and ability to enact legislation to make things happen on a large scale relatively easily. Yet time and again successful local initiatives fail to break into the mainstream. Some apparently powerful ideas championed by frontline public service managers have languished and never found sufficient backing to grow to any scale. Others are simply resisted by professional and other interests – even when there is strong evidence that they work better than existing models.

This seems to be a perennial problem, for without the ability to bring new approaches to scale, governments cannot take advantage of innovation as the most important driver of quality and relevance in public services. This is the ultimate challenge for public service innovation.

Our understanding of the challenge

Given the importance of this topic for governments, it is surprising that serious analysis of how to scale up public service innovations is still in its infancy. A survey conducted by one of this essay's authors at the beginning of the decade threw up almost no serious analyses, no consensus on a set of core accepted concepts, no datasets.

Our work at the Young Foundation on the broader field of social innovation has confirmed that this is a field with more anecdotes and promising ideas than reliable conclusions. The literature on scaling up in the public sector is currently largely fragmented into studies that focus on only one particular form of scaling up and there is a real gap in analysis of which form is best for a particular innovation. In the typology shown in table 1, we distinguish between five types of scaling up.

These five different patterns of scaling up an innovation have different traits. We will discuss here the most important distinction: methods for diffusing an idea (types 1 to 3) and methods for growing an organisation (types 4 and 5).

Diffusing an idea

Many great innovations spread in the form of an idea or concept, a set of design principles or a basic model for a new programme. The recent spread of neighbourhood policing is a good example. Diffusion occurs when others are inspired to take up the innovation for themselves and emulate the original innovator, sometimes with assistance from the originators. The research suggests that the easiest ideas to diffuse are those that are simple, observable and triallable, preferably with unambiguous advantages.

For this reason, ideas that have worked locally often need to be better codified before they can be shared. The growing service re-design movement has often found compelling ways to visually communicate key features of a new design for a service. But codification is never sufficient in itself, because there will always be tacit knowledge possessed by those involved in the original initiative

Table 1 Patterns of scaling up public service innovation

Methods for diffusing an idea

Type 1 =	General ideas and principles	Spread through advocacy, persuasion and the sense of a movement; eg the idea of prescribing holistic healthcare
Type 2 =	Type 1 + design features	Spread through professional and other networks, helped by some evaluation; eg the 'See and Treat' practice in NHS hospitals' Accident and Emergency wards
Type 3 =	Type 2 + specified programmes	Spread through professional and other networks, sometimes with payment, intellectual property, technical assistance and consultancy; eg some methadone treatment programmes for heroin addicts or the High/Scope Perry model for early years[2]

Methods for growing an organisation

Type 4 =	Type 3 + franchising	Spread by an organisation, using quality assurance, common training and other support; eg the one-third of independent public schools in Sweden that are part of a single network
Type 5 =	Type 4 + some direct control	Organic growth of a single organisation, sometimes including takeovers, with a common albeit often federated governance structure; eg the Open University

that will be picked up only on 'seeing is believing' visits by managers looking to take up the initiative. The requirement for unambiguous advantages can also be a real stumbling block. When dealing with complex social problems, different professionals may simply have different views as to what counts as success.

Public sector innovations tend to require a high level of felt ownership from the public service managers who will implement them. To achieve this, it is important that managers in different localities can tinker with the innovation to make it their own, experiment with small changes, customise it and adapt it to the local context. The relevant metaphor is 'graft and grow' not 'cut and paste'.

Getting this right is very difficult: too much adaptation to local circumstances can make scaling up barely easier than starting from scratch, or can end up as simply re-badging existing practices as everyone jumps on the bandwagon. Too little adaptation, though, can fail to foster that all important sense of local ownership, leading to failure. What's more, not all innovations stand up to this kind of tinkering. Those that rely on the presence of multiple delicately balanced and interwoven essential elements can fail when a local manager does not fully understand the interdependences they are working with. This in turn can undermine the credibility of the original idea.

One consistent finding from the research into diffusion is both obvious and particularly revealing. The innovations that most easily diffuse within a bureaucracy are those that pose least challenge to the status quo. They are the ideas that help professionals meet existing targets and objectives with minimal change or additional resources. At heart, diffusion as a method of scaling up relies on the preparedness of professionals and managers in the wider system to act as willing and active adopters of the innovation.

But unfortunately the incentives for adoption of innovation in the public sector can be very weak. Few managers are taken to task for failing to keep up with best practice in their field. Innovations may threaten demarcation lines and power structures, particularly if they cut across organisational boundaries, which will be the case for many social innovations. Few managers are very motivated by the prospect of making a saving for another manager's budget.

Growing an organisation

The other way to scale up an innovation is to embed it in a new organisation of its own and then grow the organisation itself. While this is the most prominent method in the business world – perhaps because it allows the originator to retain a share in the profits of success – it has until recently been largely neglected by those looking at public sector innovation. The benefit of growing an innovative organisation rather than diffusing an innovative idea is one factor lying behind the rise in recent years of social enterprises and the third sector more generally as providers of public services (a trend that is also linked to the trend for privatisation in previous decades).

But innovations can equally be developed by creating and scaling up new organisations that are an integral part of the public sector itself. In the 1960s Britain's Labour government created the Open University. Where all existing universities were based in a physical place this one would be virtual and would make full use of television and the telephone. Where all existing universities aimed to teach people who had just left school this one would be open to people of any age.

Most people in existing universities scoffed at the idea. There would be no demand; it wouldn't work; standards would be too low. Yet the government went ahead and today the Open University is the UK's largest provider of higher education and an acknowledged world leader in distance education (dozens of OU-inspired organisations now operate globally, from China and India to Africa). Harold Wilson, who as prime minister oversaw its creation, described it as his proudest achievement. In a survey in 2006 it also scored the highest marks of any higher education institution in terms of student satisfaction. It has expanded participation in higher education massively and made full use of new communications technologies as they came along, from satellites to the web.

Thirty years later another government introduced another radical innovation that was equally opposed by vested interests. This was a phone and web-based service that the public could call on for diagnoses, even at 3am. NHS Direct combined three existing elements in a new way: the telephone, nurses and computers with diagnostic software. Within a few years it was receiving two million calls each month and evaluations showed that its diagnoses were as reliable as doctors meeting patients face to face.

Scaling up through organisational growth can provide an easier path around some of the barriers to the diffusion of an idea. For both the Open University and NHS Direct, there was no effective motivation for professionals in the existing bureaucracies to adopt the innovations. In fact, both represented strong challenges to some very powerful vested interests and had to be built up, at least initially, outside existing structures. This is why distance learning was not pioneered by a more established university and diffused throughout the system.

A new, separate organisational structure can provide a sanctuary for an innovation, building up a strong ethos among the staff of belief in the worth of the innovation so that the inevitable teething problems are treated as such rather than excuses to kill off the initiative prematurely. A separate organisation may also be better able to build any specialist skills required for an innovation and also can also give more prominence to an innovation, generating more interest and potentially more support.

Although there are advantages to this method of scaling up, it is not without its challenges. Here we can look to the research on business innovation and growth to better understand the issues, as most of them also apply to the public sector. The best encapsulation remains James March's distinction between the modes of 'exploration' and 'exploitation'.[3] New start-ups begin in 'explorer' mode. They may be based on a real innovation, but the detail, implementation and implications of this innovation must be explored by the start-up organisation in order to prove its worth and because all innovations begin half-baked, flawed in some way and in need of refining through practical application. There is great uncertainty regarding whether the model will work and whether it will be better than existing models.

As an organisation grows and matures, it naturally moves from 'explorer' mode to 'exploiter' mode. Exploitation is about achieving maximum performance by delivering a defined model. It requires tight focus on the current agenda with all energy aimed at effective, timely execution. The characteristics of the exploiter mode can be seen just as readily in the highest-performing public service organisations as in businesses, even if the language of 'exploitation' sits less comfortably.

Organisations that manage to combine these modes and be both innovative and efficient are rare, because the different modes involve quite different tasks, organisational capabilities and typically different organisational designs. The importance of being able to follow loops and detours in the creative 'explorer' phase is eliminated as inefficiency in the 'exploiter' phase. A culture of all mucking in to solve big challenges gives way to one of taking responsibility for executing assigned tasks within a set of strongly centralised processes. Informal communication and decision-making patterns may need to be replaced with more formalised, bureaucratic ones.

All of this can be extremely disruptive at an organisational level and a hefty challenge on a personal level for the founders of the organisation. This is why in the business sector, venture capitalists typically insist on having the right to appoint the CEOs of their portfolio companies. They make frequent use of this power to replace companies' founders.[4] In the social sector, where such powers don't exist, or the public sector, where such ruthlessness is rarely seen, the result can often be 'founder syndrome', where a charismatic leader who was so beneficial for an organisation early on gradually becomes the anchor that holds it back from further development.

Diffusing an idea and growing an organisation are different ways to scale up public service innovations. Neither is better than the other overall, but most innovations will be better suited to being scaled up in one of these ways rather than the other. We should recognise that this is a choice to be made and be careful when we make it.

Organising for innovation

So far we have been looking at public service innovation from the perspective of the innovator. Public service managers, policy-makers and commissioners need to have some understanding of this perspective and should organise bureaucracies so that they are receptive to promising innovations. In short, innovation needs to become institutionalised with public services. This means that thinking about innovation has to be integrated into mainstream processes, such as strategic planning and annual spending reviews. When innovation works well it is a sign that managers and ministers are paying attention to the different horizons to which any competent organisation should be looking (see figure 5):

○ the short-term horizon of immediate problems, media and politics
○ the medium-term horizon of policies and programmes, where implementation is usually the paramount concern
○ the longer-term horizon where new policies and innovations become critical
○ and increasingly the generational horizon of issues like pensions and climate change where governments have to be looking 50 years into the future.

Any good leadership should be able to demonstrate what it is doing for each of these time horizons. And any good leadership should be able to point to a pipeline of promising innovations which could in time become mainstream. Indeed that is part of what being ready for the future means.

The public sector has a particular challenge here when compared with the private sector. Most business sectors are characterised either by stable conditions with long planning horizons (most manufacturing, oil & gas, to some extent financial services) which favour businesses that excel at the 'exploiter' traits mentioned earlier (eg Toyota, HSBC); or by fast-moving changes in technology or consumer trends (media and technology, fast-moving consumer goods) that favour more 'explorer' traits even in mature organisations (eg Nokia, Apple, 3M). The public sector faces a need to drive large-scale operations like tax collection, often of a fairly routine kind, but where failure to deliver can have devastating consequences for people's lives. But it needs to prepare simultaneously for radically different challenges such as climate change.

Figure 5 The timescales for decision, action and results

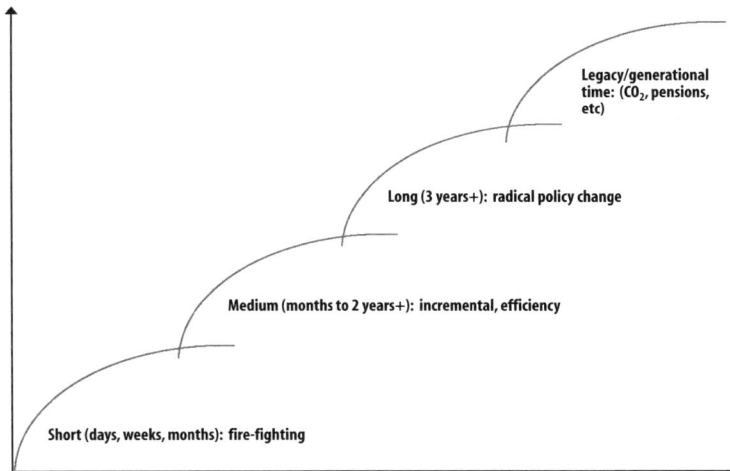

Legacy/generational time: (CO_2, pensions, etc)

Long (3 years+): radical policy change

Medium (months to 2 years+): incremental, efficiency

Short (days, weeks, months): fire-fighting

Dedicated centres of innovation

In organising for innovation, this need to combine explorer and exploiter traits means that a certain amount needs to be done to incorporate innovation into mainstream decision-making, but that the most impact may be achieved by parts of the bureaucracy that are entirely dedicated to innovation. Apple does not have such innovation units, for example, because the entire company seeks to be innovative, but this can result not just in successes such as the iPod, but failures such as the Newton that would be unacceptable in the public sector.

Some governments have made tentative steps in this direction.

Denmark's Ministry of Finance, for instance, has set up a unit to promote new ideas – like plans to create a single account for financial transactions with citizens. The Ministry of Economics and Business Affairs has restructured itself to be based much more on projects than functions and has established its own internal consultancy, MindLab, to promote creativity.[5] In Finland, the main technology agency, SITRA, has turned its attention to public sector innovation.

In the USA, Minnesota for a time had an innovation unit and until recently even the US State Department had a Center for Administrative Innovation. Singapore has promoted innovations through its Enterprise Challenge programme, run through the Prime Minister's office, which has funded some 68 proposals at a cost of over $11 million, such as a 'virtual policing centre' for non-urgent enquiries to be routed through to the Singapore Police Force, and teleconferencing for prison inmates to interact with their relatives. It claims these could achieve savings ten times greater than their costs. Others countries, including Brazil, Denmark, South Africa and the USA, have introduced official awards for public innovators.

The UK has never had equivalent champions for innovation in the public sector. But it has nevertheless experimented with ways of opening up the bureaucracy. There have been experiments to liberate local managers to break national rules – including the short-lived education and health action zones, and the now well-established employment zones. The 'Invest to Save' budget provided a large pool of money to back promising innovations that crossed organisational boundaries. The Department for Education set up an innovation unit which has supported imaginative communities of practice and administers the 'power to innovate', a provision that allows the Department to de-apply any education legislation for the purposes of running a trial of an innovative programme. The Department of Health has established an NHS Institute for Innovation and Improvement. Within individual agencies, too, smaller innovation funds have been used widely to give frontline managers a chance to try out new ideas. Going further means paying greater attention to the following factors.

Culture and leadership

Leaders within the public sector need to signal that innovation matters: awards and prizes can help by providing recognition, as can promoting people who have carried through an important innovation. There needs to be someone at board level in departments and agencies responsible for innovation, including scaling up the successes.

Networks

One of the important insights that comes out of many studies of individual innovations is that formal organisational structures count for less than people and relationships. It is the alignment of a group of key people – an official, outside experts and advisers, a minister – that helps to take an idea to fruition. Champions who can span organisational and disciplinary boundaries are especially important since many innovations cut across traditional structures.

Commissioning

Where the route to scaling up an innovation is through growth of an organisation, the role of public service commissioners comes to the fore. Our two example organisations mentioned earlier, the Open University and NHS Direct, are notable in that neither had to rely on winning contracts in order to grow, which vastly simplified things. Most organisations do not have this luxury and rely on being commissioned to provide a service by one public body or another.

There is a strong case for public service commissioners treating innovative projects quite differently from the norm. As we have discussed, innovations proved on a local scale will still need to be refined and adapted to work on a regional or national scale. This means that the growing organisation needs to retain some of the characteristic behaviours of an 'explorer' even as it gradually adopts 'exploiter' traits.

As a result, opportunities to learn through quick planning iterations should be built into the commissioning arrangements from the outset. Once a plan has been agreed within a typical project, the project leaders often view their duty as implementing the plan as stated and delivering the expected results. If they fall behind, the conditioned response may often be to keep a low profile while working twice as hard, hoping to get back on track. This response can be disastrous for scaling up innovations, however, because it brings learning to a halt.

Leaders attempting to scale up innovative projects must be given the assurance that their commissioners understand that the plan is based on relatively high levels of uncertainty and that the goal is to learn and adapt as quickly as possible. These leaders should be encouraged to go out of their way to demonstrate the quality of their thought processes. This has implications for the budget and timescale for innovative projects.

The metrics used to track how innovations are performing need careful thought, recognising that the early results may be misleading, and recognising too the very different timescales for different kinds of innovation. There is a vast difference between a new programme that can be implemented within a year or two (like choice in hospital treatments) and a new culture that may take a decade to take shape. This is also where the mantra of evidence-based government can be misleading. A classic example is the spate of programmes, like High/Scope Perry, to help young children that were launched in the US in the 1960s. For ten years or so the evaluations of these programmes were generally negative. It was only later that it became clear that these could achieve impressive paybacks in terms of better education and lower crime. The same may be happening to the UK's Sure Start programme, whose first evaluation was equally ambiguous.

The importance of joined-up commissioning among public service organisations, reducing the administrative burden and clarifying the targets placed on boundary-crossing innovations, is now well established among policy-makers in the UK, although implementing this in practice can prove very difficult.

Handling risks

At every stage in the innovation process there are risks. Right from the start, even a small-scale pilot may be looked at as a signal of where government wants to take policy. If it fails, ministers will be called to account for wasted money. If people's lives are damaged the voters will justifiably be angry.

So any programme of innovation has to be smart about risks and how they should be managed. Generally it will be easier to take risks where everyone agrees that things aren't working. It will also be easier if government is honest that it is experimenting with a range of options, rather than pretending that all will succeed. It will be easier where users have choice (so that they can choose a radically different model of school or doctor rather than having it forced on them), and it will be easier where the innovation is managed by an organisation at one remove from the state, a business or NGO, so that if things go wrong they can take the blame. The key is to be explicit about risks and how they should be managed. It will also be easier if projects can be placed within a portfolio, spreading the risk and providing a success story for the overall portfolio even if individual projects go awry.

For more detail see the NESTA publication by Geoff Mulgan, *Ready or Not: Taking public sector innovation seriously.*[6]

Geoff Mulgan is director and Simon Tucker is associate director, Young Foundation.

Notes

1   B Nooteboom, *Learning and Innovation in Organisations and Economies* (Oxford: Oxford University Press, 2000).
2   See for instance www.childtrends.org/Lifecourse/programs/HighScope-PerryPreschoolProgram.htm (accessed 24 Jun 2007).
3   J March, 'Exploration and exploitation in organisational learning', *Organisational Science* 2 (1991).
4   T Hellmann, 'The allocation of control rights in venture capital contracts', *RAND Journal of Economics* 29 (1998).
5   National Audit Office, *Achieving Innovation in Central Government*

Organizations (London: TSO, Jul 2006), available at www.nao.org.uk/
publications/nao_reports/05-06/05061447i.pdf (accessed 12 Jun 2007).

6   G Mulgan, *Ready or Not: Taking public sector innovation seriously* (London:
National Endowment for Science, Technology and the Arts, 2007).

13. Seven kinds of learning

How governments should translate innovation into action

Tom Bentley

When we look back at 2007 in the decades to come, we may recognise it as the year that climate change finally broke into the international political mainstream. The combination of the British government's Stern Review,[1] the Fourth Assessment report of the Inter-governmental Panel on Climate Change (IPCC)[2] and Al Gore's Oscar for *An Inconvenient Truth* pushed the issue to the forefront of the global imagination.

The climate change debate is decades old, but political action quickly followed these three interventions. In March 2007, the European Union made a unilateral commitment to cut its CO_2 emissions by 20 per cent against 1990 levels and to generate 20 per cent of its energy from renewable sources by 2020. Britain introduced its own climate change bill, with legally binding targets for emissions reduction. Australian state governments agreed to develop a National Emissions Trading Scheme, whether or not their federal government joins in. New policy developments are making news on a weekly basis.

This is often how processes of learning in government begin. Different kinds of information and narrative are marshalled – Gore's personal story, Stern's economic calculations, the IPCC's dense scientific evidence – and together they create a popular, political and technical case for a major shift in policy. But has this breaking policy wave actually had any impact on carbon emissions, or on the capacity of governments to influence how people respond to a warming world?

In truth, we are only one step further in an ongoing saga. We cannot move to a low carbon economy in a flash of evidence-based inspiration. The process of change will require deep, fast, radical innovation to develop new possibilities. But new ideas are worthwhile only when they can be translated into better outcomes for society as a whole. So governments also need to learn from innovations and to apply that learning systematically across and beyond public institutions.

In this essay, I examine the ways in which governments can develop the kind of effective learning capacity that will enable them to respond not just to climate change, but to a range of major challenges over the coming decades.

Learning in systems

Making policy is only one part of the whole system of government – its success depends on its ability to both effect and respond to changes in behaviour by many organisations within the public sector itself and, more importantly, beyond government – among citizens, firms and non-governmental organisations.

Gathering the knowledge for a defensible policy consensus is one task. Mobilising a response which actually influences the path of economic, institutional and environmental development – at sufficient depth, within the right timescale, and without creating unacceptable side-effects – is far more complex.

When it comes to climate change, some of the potential lines of action have been clear for some time: introducing a price for carbon, and market systems that enable emissions permits and savings to be traded. The challenge now is not to generate ideas, but to choose, implement and learn from them. This is particularly true when we consider the knock-on implications of environmental policy innovation for infrastructure investment, planning, security, public behaviour and so on.

As the list of actions, and their possible impacts, spreads out, it becomes clear how many different kinds of knowledge and capability are involved in generating any effective response to climate change. That is why the challenge of learning in government involves learning within *systems*.

Governments can be easily fooled by their own organisational charts into believing that learning and action follow well-defined chains of command. Bringing about new behaviour in the light of fresh experience, evidence and commitments is often treated either as a simple matter of making new information available or creating incentives so that it is rational for people to change their behaviour.

In reality, the most influential learning is often transmitted through informal networks – both within government and in the wider arena, between all organisations. Change is therefore more likely to happen if we work out how to create learning systems that work to transfer knowledge, innovation and capability across different organisations, recognising that different bodies will learn differently.

Given these dynamics, the overall learning of governments should be seen, not so much as adjusting and refining policy positions in the light of new information, but more as 'adaptive reorganisation within complex systems'.[3] The meaning of 'adaptive' reflects Ronald Heifetz's definition: adaptive change goes beyond what is technically possible within current options, and is directed towards a longer-term purpose or goal.[4]

'What's next?' How governments make decisions

Unfortunately, the structures and processes of many governments make it very hard to achieve this translation of innovation into action. This is ironic, since governments are actually built around the processing of information and house huge concentrations of knowledge. But understanding *how* they take decisions and why this impacts on their ability to learn systemically, is crucial to overcoming the obstacles.

In the television drama *The West Wing* President Josiah Bartlett famously uses the question 'What's next?' as his primary tool of management. It means 'the discussion is over', and reflects the range of issues and viewpoints facing an executive decision-maker and their potential to become overwhelming.

The idea that government is structured around functional 'silos' that house specialist knowledge and control their resources jealously is very familiar. Less obvious is that governments coordinate themselves by maintaining a series of *routines*. Given the range of continuous demands and functions, the only way to make reliable, legitimate, effective decisions is to maintain consistent rules and routines about how they are taken. Bureaucratic proceduralism might occasionally drive us mad, but it is rooted in an inescapable need.

As Glyn Davis explains, the centre of government is the place where three kinds of coordinating routine come together: political, policy and administrative.[5] Davis was focusing on the premier's or prime minister's function, which he helped to build in the Australian state of Queensland; I would include budget coordination in the list, given the importance of budgets to structuring how the whole of government works.

Every aspect of government rests on such routines in some way. Manifestations of them include cabinet decision-making, budgeting, spending, statistical reporting, regulatory reviews, which are built into the permanent cycle of governance, and elections, which create a routine for the formation and dissolution of governments.

Managing these routines is how governments handle their many conflicting tasks and pressures. But routines can easily take on a life of their own. If different cycles are not carefully connected with each other, they separate actions and activities in ways which impede the flow of learning across whole systems. An obvious example is the way that different departments within a government often maintain different information management systems, and thus staff in one department rarely know what their colleagues know. Another is the way that budget processes focus attention on the new money to be allocated, but rarely examine the allocation or the impact of funding which has already been allocated and makes up the bulk of current activity.

Governments cannot translate innovation into results unless they work out how to learn from the experience of trying to implement their own policies, or apply new learning to existing activity. Recurring decisions need to be influenced by fresh experience, new intelligence and new commitments if learning in government is to succeed.

Seven kinds of learning

The need to break policy decisions down into manageable chunks and tackle them separately reinforces our tendency to view learning as a matter of rationally bringing information and evidence to bear on an individual decision at a specific moment. This idea, encapsulated in the idea of 'briefing' decision-makers and minuting their decisions, dominates the formal processes of government business.

Of course, the intelligence and analysis embodied in the best policy processes is an essential component of knowledge. But the idea that we are rational and evidence-based only in our approach to decisions reinforces the pervasive gap between knowing and doing which so many large organisations suffer from. If we want to learn effectively across systems, we need to recognise that there are several kinds of learning which occur in governments all the time. Below are seven which I believe are especially important.

Imitation

The first is the most neglected form of social learning: imitation. Most of us adopt a new phrase, idea or behaviour when we see other people using it in ways that we want to emulate. Media and marketing provide a mass vehicle for this practice, but its origins lie in our genetic history, and our behaviour in organisations is no different.

Since the democratic process is a competition for power, and the process of government is an internal competition for power and resources, people are very likely to imitate practices and methods that have proved successful in influencing what government does. For example, in the UK, when the Performance and Innovation Unit was first established in the Cabinet Office in 2001, few people understood or noticed. Five years later, there are strategy units across most Whitehall departments and in central agencies around the world.

Competitive politics makes imitation integral to government. While furiously seeking points of difference and distinction, opposition parties are also working out how to emulate the characteristics of successful governments. Tony Blair won by neutralising the Conservatives on economic management and crime; Fredrik Reinfeld beat the Swedish Social Democrats by abandoning his party's commitment to shrinking the state.

International comparison is a powerful source of learning, or at least a stimulus to learning. But comparison is not the same as imitation; working out what to imitate from a statistical table is much harder than observing the impact of specific behaviours in practice. That is one reason why genuine learning between different systems of governance is usually preceded by years of debate and discussion.

Iteration

Not all policies can be fully implemented in a single stroke. Because discretionary spending arrives in small slices, and politicians have many interests to reflect, many new approaches emerge through a series of incremental steps.

The UK tax credit system is an example of repeated iteration with learning successes and failures attached. It was introduced early in the life of a new government and presented as a major structural reform. But its development has come through annual adjustments, extensions and refinements, both in its scope and its methods.

The system was subject to extensive economic modelling by the Treasury, but it underestimated the effect that complexity of administration and application would have on uptake, and failed to foresee the impact of clawing back overpayment from families who had already spent the money.

These errors highlighted the flaws of assuming economic rationality in personal behaviour, but also show the difficulty of modelling systemic changes for large numbers of people. Nonetheless, the tax credit system has developed into a far more comprehensive and integrated framework for processing taxes and income subsidies than when it was first introduced; and it has taken time to allow learning.

Using repeated, practical iterations for designing, developing and scaling up new methods and service delivery models in public services is now emerging as a potent source of accelerated learning. Rather than debating the merits of a model in the abstract, and then seeking to deliver it through an existing institutional channel, this approach offers greater openness to innovation combined with greater capacity for learning from one iteration to another.

Migration

Partly because imitation is so powerful, much learning travels with people rather than in documents. Much of what governments need to learn is situational; much of what public servants know is acquired through their experience and never formally articulated or recorded. It follows that the flow of people around and between organisations, in and out of government, is one of the most influential sources of learning.

The most frequent replacement takes place at the top, but the intermediate layers are probably even more important for government as a whole. In general, the movement of people between sectors and organisations during their career has increased. But vertical career progression within government is still far better understood than lateral movement and the networks of knowledge exchange that it can create. If outsiders are deliberately imported and given the task of 'being different', for example by being put in charge of 'innovation', they will be isolated and neutralised by a host culture.

Improvisation

Some of the most powerful learning experiences can come from having to act in circumstances where you do not know exactly what to do. Often, governments make commitments that they do not know how to implement. It can be the pressure of a target that leads to new responses, like a 60 per cent reduction in carbon dioxide emissions, or it can be the onset of new and unexpected conditions, like the September 11th attacks.

Often, when circumstances require new responses, governments reach for ones that they recognise or have confidence in. Donald Rumsfeld's advocacy of invasion of Iraq might count as such: an old plan for tackling a new problem which has proved unfit for the conditions, and implemented by people who are incapable of understanding their own role in creating those conditions.

But if governments are more able to acknowledge uncertainty, and to manage their risks by diversifying their range of options rather than reducing their level of commitment, they have more chance of uncovering genuinely useful tools and approaches that they can use more widely.

Interpretation

As the use of contracts and third party government has grown, so has the systematic use of audit, inspection and formal evaluation. Commissioning independent evaluations of performance is one of the most important sources of challenge and information to governments. The recent Unicef report on children's quality of life,[6] for example, had a similar impact in the UK to the Rowntree Foundation's inquiry on income and wealth in the mid-1990s in bringing new issues of social and public failure to light.

Governments often reject such findings or deny their validity, but if they are verified and produce a public reaction they are likely to force a level of response which goes beyond the existing repertoire. But simply conducting evaluation exercises does not in itself lead to learning. Converting evaluation successfully into innovation depends not just on mastery of the technical detail. As Richard Lester and Michael Piore explain, capitalising on innovation requires a sustained capacity for interpretation of results which contain a high degree of uncertainty. Dealing with ambiguity and partial information, and remaining open to different interpretations without losing long-term direction, is therefore essential to cumulative learning.[7]

Storytelling

Our receptiveness to narrative, and the ability to absorb and relate a story about identifiable characters to our own experiences and capabilities, also arises from our evolution. Stories are therefore one of the most powerful ways to communicate lessons, and make them portable, though they suffer from other weaknesses as vehicles of learning.

For governments, stories also act as a way to communicate more abstract, diffuse messages. All governments are now increasingly concerned with crafting their 'narrative' as opposed to a series of disjointed 'messages'. Many governments, however, fail to find stories that are genuinely helpful in communicating their wider sense of purpose: halfway through Tony Blair's government New Labour was still struggling to tell a story that people could understand and act on.

This is a crucial failing for a government whose public service goals depended on mobilising millions of workers and tens of millions of users. In contrast, for several decades Mexican public health agencies have been successfully influencing the behaviour of millions of illiterate citizens through radio soap operas covering pregnancy, sexual health and domestic violence storylines.

Unfortunately for many individual politicians, media culture and public interest are more likely to be focused on stories about their personal lives than the 'official script' they offer as an account of their public actions. Organisational storytelling is also a crucially important vehicle for spreading learning across the many layers and locations of large institutions; used well, it can provide a sense of coherence and purpose not imparted by other tools of management.

Evolution: government as learning system

The final kind of learning is the most important and the most difficult. Combining all these different activities, at different levels, into cumulative patterns of learning requires a different view of how government operates.

Many efforts to learn in government focus, understandably, on the attempt to isolate one question and answer it definitively in a way that shows what the policy should be and what the agencies in question should do. As I have argued, this tendency is reinforced by the design of modern bureaucracies into manageable chunks, by the economists' use of assumptions to screen out behavioural complexity, and by the natural scientists' desire for 'control conditions' under which experimental results can be verified.

Unfortunately, the areas of government action under which any of these conditions holds is strictly limited. Instead, government has to operate as part of an increasingly interconnected set of relationships in perpetual motion. While the sources of real-time information are far better than a decade ago, they never provide a complete picture. Instead, participants in governments are also participants in overlapping and incomplete learning processes and relationships.

My argument has been that government should use its own reliance on repeated cycles of activity to introduce manageable time horizons and iterative learning opportunities directly into both policy development and implementation. Systematising this perspective means treating government, and the wider systems it seeks to influence, as evolutionary systems. Evolution advances through a continuous, multilevel process of trial and error. The further it advances, the more complex and diverse the range of activity it can sustain.

The evolutionary metaphor is often misunderstood and oversimplified; it does not imply a war of all against all for survival. But it does imply continuous adaptation and adjustment by many autonomous participants in interdependent relationships.

Biological evolution has no conscious purpose; it emerges from the single urge to reproduce. Governments, by contrast, have many conflicting purposes. Working out how to handle conflicting ends and means is part of the essence of government. The way to turn evolution into evolutionary learning is to set the continuous, open-ended processes against the goals and outcomes for which governments are accountable to citizens.

Under this model, we should give up trying to imagine all the elements and actions tied together under the banner of government as part of one single, intentional chain of logic. Instead, it may be better to recognise that government consists of many different identities and purposes, competing and collaborating across many different levels and subsystems, adapting to changing conditions and occasionally leaving behind practices and organisations which no longer fit.

It also helps to make sense of the role that networks can play in enabling governments to learn better; they allow faster 'co-evolution' between different jurisdictions, regulators and firms, governments and oppositions, separate divisions, researchers and practitioners, because they allow direct, real-time communication across locations and organisational boundaries. Such networks do not replace the hierarchical architecture of government, but wrap around it, creating new shortcuts and allowing new patterns of collaboration.

Under these kinds of conditions, the capacity of governments to learn systemically therefore depends on linking and aligning the multiple layers of government activity with the flow of experience and innovation that arises from the seven kinds of learning. There is no template or blueprint for doing this scientifically, but it is possible to pursue it rigorously from many different locations in government.

In analysing the properties of successful innovation systems, Australian researchers Jonathan West and Keith Smith argue that such systems embody five distinct functions:[8]

O   identifying opportunities
O   creating and distributing knowledge and capabilities
O   supporting and financing new organisations and production capacities
O   managing risk and uncertainty
O   creating and managing infrastructures, for example transport and communication.

They argue that successful national innovation systems develop all of these functions, and link them together across sectoral, geographical and organisational boundaries. I would suggest that the same functions combined help to make up the learning systems that governments increasingly need.

To succeed in the twenty-first century, governments will need to learn faster and more deeply from innovation. They can do this without changing their core identities – by working out how to learn continuously through the iterative cycles of their ongoing routines, rather than simply making incremental steps forward; by deliberately creating feedback loops that help integrate new decisions and resources with the whole that already exists; by building 'search networks' capable of identifying learning objectives and searching systematically across organisational boundaries for relevant knowledge and intelligence; and by recognising, building and rewarding adaptive capacity in the organisations they fund and regulate.

Judging what to do on the basis of imperfect information is the essence of both political and organisational leadership. Those leaders who build learning systems around their routines will be the ones who do most to help reinvent government for the twenty-first century.

Tom Bentley is an executive director in the Department of Premier and Cabinet in the State Government of Victoria, Australia, and director of applied learning at ANZSOG, the Australia and New Zealand School of Government. He writes here in a personal capacity.

Notes

1   See 'Stern review on the economics of climate change', Oct 2006, available at www.hm-treasury.gov.uk/independent_reviews/stern_review_economics_ climate_change/stern_review_report.cfm (accessed 12 Jun 2007).
2   See Intergovernmental Panel on Climate Change, *Climate Change 2007: The physical science basis* (IPCC: Geneva, Feb 2007), available at www.ipcc.ch/SPM2feb07.pdf (accessed 12 Jun 2007).
3   D North, *Understanding the Process of Economic Change* (Princeton: Princeton University Press, 2005).
4   R Heifetz, 'Adaptive work' in T Bentley and J Wilsdon (eds), *The Adaptive State: Strategies for personalising the public realm* (London: Demos, 2003).

5   G Davis, *A Government of Routines: Executive coordination in an Australian state* (Melbourne: Centre for Australian Public Sector Management, 1995).

6   Unicef, *Child Poverty in Perspective: An overview of child wellbeing in rich countries* (Florence: Unicef, 2007), available at http://news.bbc.co.uk/nol/shared/bsp/hi/pdfs/13_02_07_nn_unicef.pdf (accessed 18 Jun 2007).

7   R Lester and M Piore, *Innovation: The missing dimension* (Boston: Harvard University Press, 2004).

8   J West and K Smith, 'Australia's innovation challenges: building an effective national innovation system', *Melbourne Business Review*, Oct 2005.

DEMOS – Licence to Publish

THE WORK (AS DEFINED BELOW) IS PROVIDED UNDER THE TERMS OF THIS LICENCE ("LICENCE"). THE WORK IS PROTECTED BY COPYRIGHT AND/OR OTHER APPLICABLE LAW. ANY USE OF THE WORK OTHER THAN AS AUTHORIZED UNDER THIS LICENCE IS PROHIBITED. BY EXERCISING ANY RIGHTS TO THE WORK PROVIDED HERE, YOU ACCEPT AND AGREE TO BE BOUND BY THE TERMS OF THIS LICENCE. DEMOS GRANTS YOU THE RIGHTS CONTAINED HERE IN CONSIDERATION OF YOUR ACCEPTANCE OF SUCH TERMS AND CONDITIONS.

1. **Definitions**
   a **"Collective Work"** means a work, such as a periodical issue, anthology or encyclopedia, in which the Work in its entirety in unmodified form, along with a number of other contributions, constituting separate and independent works in themselves, are assembled into a collective whole. A work that constitutes a Collective Work will not be considered a Derivative Work (as defined below) for the purposes of this Licence.
   b **"Derivative Work"** means a work based upon the Work or upon the Work and other pre-existing works, such as a musical arrangement, dramatization, fictionalization, motion picture version, sound recording, art reproduction, abridgment, condensation, or any other form in which the Work may be recast, transformed, or adapted, except that a work that constitutes a Collective Work or a translation from English into another language will not be considered a Derivative Work for the purpose of this Licence.
   c **"Licensor"** means the individual or entity that offers the Work under the terms of this Licence.
   d **"Original Author"** means the individual or entity who created the Work.
   e **"Work"** means the copyrightable work of authorship offered under the terms of this Licence.
   f **"You"** means an individual or entity exercising rights under this Licence who has not previously violated the terms of this Licence with respect to the Work, or who has received express permission from DEMOS to exercise rights under this Licence despite a previous violation.
2. **Fair Use Rights.** Nothing in this licence is intended to reduce, limit, or restrict any rights arising from fair use, first sale or other limitations on the exclusive rights of the copyright owner under copyright law or other applicable laws.
3. **Licence Grant.** Subject to the terms and conditions of this Licence, Licensor hereby grants You a worldwide, royalty-free, non-exclusive, perpetual (for the duration of the applicable copyright) licence to exercise the rights in the Work as stated below:
   a to reproduce the Work, to incorporate the Work into one or more Collective Works, and to reproduce the Work as incorporated in the Collective Works;
   b to distribute copies or phonorecords of, display publicly, perform publicly, and perform publicly by means of a digital audio transmission the Work including as incorporated in Collective Works;
   The above rights may be exercised in all media and formats whether now known or hereafter devised. The above rights include the right to make such modifications as are technically necessary to exercise the rights in other media and formats. All rights not expressly granted by Licensor are hereby reserved.
4. **Restrictions.** The licence granted in Section 3 above is expressly made subject to and limited by the following restrictions:
   a You may distribute, publicly display, publicly perform, or publicly digitally perform the Work only under the terms of this Licence, and You must include a copy of, or the Uniform Resource Identifier for, this Licence with every copy or phonorecord of the Work You distribute, publicly display, publicly perform, or publicly digitally perform. You may not offer or impose any terms on the Work that alter or restrict the terms of this Licence or the recipients' exercise of the rights granted hereunder. You may not sublicence the Work. You must keep intact all notices that refer to this Licence and to the disclaimer of warranties. You may not distribute, publicly display, publicly perform, or publicly digitally perform the Work with any technological measures that control access or use of the Work in a manner inconsistent with the terms of this Licence Agreement. The above applies to the Work as incorporated in a Collective Work, but this does not require the Collective Work apart from the Work itself to be made subject to the terms of this Licence. If You create a Collective Work, upon notice from any Licencor You must, to the extent practicable, remove from the Collective Work any reference to such Licensor or the Original Author, as requested.

b You may not exercise any of the rights granted to You in Section 3 above in any manner that is primarily intended for or directed toward commercial advantage or private monetary compensation. The exchange of the Work for other copyrighted works by means of digital file-sharing or otherwise shall not be considered to be intended for or directed toward commercial advantage or private monetary compensation, provided there is no payment of any monetary compensation in connection with the exchange of copyrighted works.

c If you distribute, publicly display, publicly perform, or publicly digitally perform the Work or any Collective Works, You must keep intact all copyright notices for the Work and give the Original Author credit reasonable to the medium or means You are utilizing by conveying the name (or pseudonym if applicable) of the Original Author if supplied; the title of the Work if supplied. Such credit may be implemented in any reasonable manner; provided, however, that in the case of a Collective Work, at a minimum such credit will appear where any other comparable authorship credit appears and in a manner at least as prominent as such other comparable authorship credit.

5. Representations, Warranties and Disclaimer

a By offering the Work for public release under this Licence, Licensor represents and warrants that, to the best of Licensor's knowledge after reasonable inquiry:

  i Licensor has secured all rights in the Work necessary to grant the licence rights hereunder and to permit the lawful exercise of the rights granted hereunder without You having any obligation to pay any royalties, compulsory licence fees, residuals or any other payments;

  ii The Work does not infringe the copyright, trademark, publicity rights, common law rights or any other right of any third party or constitute defamation, invasion of privacy or other tortious injury to any third party.

b EXCEPT AS EXPRESSLY STATED IN THIS LICENCE OR OTHERWISE AGREED IN WRITING OR REQUIRED BY APPLICABLE LAW, THE WORK IS LICENCED ON AN "AS IS" BASIS, WITHOUT WARRANTIES OF ANY KIND, EITHER EXPRESS OR IMPLIED INCLUDING, WITHOUT LIMITATION, ANY WARRANTIES REGARDING THE CONTENTS OR ACCURACY OF THE WORK.

6. Limitation on Liability. EXCEPT TO THE EXTENT REQUIRED BY APPLICABLE LAW, AND EXCEPT FOR DAMAGES ARISING FROM LIABILITY TO A THIRD PARTY RESULTING FROM BREACH OF THE WARRANTIES IN SECTION 5, IN NO EVENT WILL LICENSOR BE LIABLE TO YOU ON ANY LEGAL THEORY FOR ANY SPECIAL, INCIDENTAL, CONSEQUENTIAL, PUNITIVE OR EXEMPLARY DAMAGES ARISING OUT OF THIS LICENCE OR THE USE OF THE WORK, EVEN IF LICENSOR HAS BEEN ADVISED OF THE POSSIBILITY OF SUCH DAMAGES.

7. Termination

a This Licence and the rights granted hereunder will terminate automatically upon any breach by You of the terms of this Licence. Individuals or entities who have received Collective Works from You under this Licence, however, will not have their licences terminated provided such individuals or entities remain in full compliance with those licences. Sections 1, 2, 5, 6, 7, and 8 will survive any termination of this Licence.

b Subject to the above terms and conditions, the licence granted here is perpetual (for the duration of the applicable copyright in the Work). Notwithstanding the above, Licensor reserves the right to release the Work under different licence terms or to stop distributing the Work at any time; provided, however that any such election will not serve to withdraw this Licence (or any other licence that has been, or is required to be, granted under the terms of this Licence), and this Licence will continue in full force and effect unless terminated as stated above.

8. Miscellaneous

a Each time You distribute or publicly digitally perform the Work or a Collective Work, DEMOS offers to the recipient a licence to the Work on the same terms and conditions as the licence granted to You under this Licence.

b If any provision of this Licence is invalid or unenforceable under applicable law, it shall not affect the validity or enforceability of the remainder of the terms of this Licence, and without further action by the parties to this agreement, such provision shall be reformed to the minimum extent necessary to make such provision valid and enforceable.

c No term or provision of this Licence shall be deemed waived and no breach consented to unless such waiver or consent shall be in writing and signed by the party to be charged with such waiver or consent.

d This Licence constitutes the entire agreement between the parties with respect to the Work licensed here. There are no understandings, agreements or representations with respect to the Work not specified here. Licensor shall not be bound by any additional provisions that may appear in any communication from You. This Licence may not be modified without the mutual written agreement of DEMOS and You.